Mark Twain in Japan

Mark Twain and His Circle Series
Tom Quirk, editor

Mark Twain in Japan

The Cultural Reception of an American Icon

Tsuyoshi Ishihara

University of Missouri Press
Columbia and London

University of Missouri Press, Columbia, Missouri 65201
Printed and bound in the United States of America

First paperback printing, 2011
5 4 3 2 1 15 14 13 12 11

Library of Congress Cataloging-in-Publication Data

Ishihara, Tsuyoshi, 1971–
Mark Twain in Japan : the cultural reception of an American icon / Tsuyoshi Ishihara.
p. cm. — (Mark Twain and his circle series)
Summary: "Explores the history of Mark Twain's reception in Japan in the spheres of books, children's magazines, and anime, the impact of Japanese translations on Twain's public image, how Japanese culture has transformed Japanese versions of Twain's works, and how Japan is culturally influenced by America and America by Japan"—Provided by publisher.
Includes bibliographical references and index.
ISBN 978-0-8262-1961-9 (pbk.:alk. paper)
1. Twain, Mark, 1835–1910—Appreciation—Japan. 2. Twain, Mark, 1835–1910—Translations into Japanese—History and criticism. 3. American literature—Appreciation—Japan. 4. Japanese literature—American influences. 5. Books and reading—Japan—History. 6. Criticism—Japan—History. I. Title. II. Series.
PS1337.4.J37I84 2005
818'.409—dc22

2005006340

∞™ This paper meets the requirements of the American National Standard for Permanence of Paper for Printed Library Materials, Z39.48, 1984.

Designer: Jennifer Cropp
Typesetter: Crane Composition, Inc.
Printer and binder: The Maple-Vail Book Manufacturing Group
Typefaces: Minion, Ruach, and Galliard

To my wife, Noriko, *with love*

Contents

Preface

This project evolved more than ten years ago when I was an undergraduate student in Japan. Although I had not yet read many American books, it was almost impossible to live in Tokyo without having contact with American culture. America was everywhere. If you walked in the streets of downtown Tokyo, you could find advertisements for American movies everywhere and hear American pop songs as background music in a variety of places. You could watch American news programs on satellite television. You could even go to Disneyland by way of an easy 40-minute train ride from downtown Tokyo. At that time, I was one of many young Japanese who were "uncritically" fascinated with almost everything about America. In my eyes, America was the country that was free from many negative aspects of Japanese culture as I saw it, such as age hierarchy, sexism, conservatism, traditionalism, snobbism, homogeneity, and so forth.

I was an English major, and even in literary works I was looking for something "distinctively American," different from my own country.

Naturally, one day I picked up the distinctively American novel *Adventures of Huckleberry Finn,* by Mark Twain. Since I knew that it was written in colloquial American English and that even American children can read this novel, I decided to read it in English, thinking I would easily understand it. However, once I started reading it, I immediately realized that I was wrong. First, the "colloquial" language of this novel was not easy at all for a Japanese student like me. I encountered unknown words and expressions on almost every page and I had to look them up in various kinds of dictionaries. Even so, I was so amazed with this novel in so many ways that I could not quit it in the middle. Although it must be unimaginable for American readers, it took me an entire three months to finish this novel. *Huckleberry Finn* became the first long novel in English that I read from cover to cover outside of the books assigned in my literature classes.

Huckleberry Finn satisfied my desire to read something distinctively American. I was fascinated with its language, humor, and, above all, its descriptions of life and nature along the Mississippi. I was surprised to find that many aspects of this novel are truly universal. Twain satirized such elements as conservatism, snobbism, and traditionalism among American southern quasi-aristocrats, negative elements I could easily find in Japan as well. Moreover, *Huckleberry Finn* vividly showed me the dark side of America in its portrayals of racism, child abuse, murder, and lynching. These were absolutely different from the "democratic" images of America that I innocently held at the time. I was impressed with this novel even more because it realistically depicted universal problems without losing its "American" flavor. In spite of those descriptions of dreadful aspects of American society, I still felt that the character of Huck seemed to represent the best part of America. He has been my greatest democratic American hero since the day I finished the novel. Naturally, I selected Mark Twain's literature as the main subject of my study in graduate school. After publishing several Japanese essays on Twain, I crossed the Pacific to devote more study to Twain and American culture.

Now I have been studying Mark Twain for almost ten years. The more I studied Twain, the more I felt fortunate about the way I first encountered his work. At the same time, however, I also began to suspect that Japanese people encountered Twain's writing in quite different ways. Undoubtedly, most Japanese were introduced to his works through Japanese translations and adaptations. How were those versions different from Twain's originals? And if they were different, why? This book evolved from these simple and genuine questions, and the following chapters contain some of the answers I have found.

Acknowledgments

This project could not have come to fruition without the generous assistance of many individuals and institutions. Thanks are due first to Prof. Shelley Fisher Fishkin, the great Twain scholar and Americanist, for her encouragement, suggestions, care, and patience. Her encyclopedic knowledge and sparkling insights were vital in developing this project. Certainly, no student of Twain can imagine a better adviser. I would also like to thank the members of my dissertation committee at the University of Texas at Austin, Professors Susan J. Napier, Janet M. Davis, Mark C. Smith, and Julia L. Mickenberg, for giving me valuable advice in shaping my ideas about this project. Various Japanese scholars also provided important materials and information. I am extremely grateful to my former advisers at Kyoto University, Professors Hirokuni Kobatake and Masugi Shimada, for their kind support and care over the course of several years. I am also very thankful to Prof. Takashi Sasaki at Doshisha University for his encouragement to continue my studies on Twain in the United States. I owe special thanks as well to Prof. Masago Igawa, former chief editor of the *Journal of Mark Twain Studies* in Japan, and Nobuo Hara at Nan'undo Publishing Co., Ltd., for permission to reprint the cover of their journal. I also wish to thank Fumiko Sakashita and Professors Makoto Nagawara, Yorimasa Nasu, and Koutaro Nakagaki for sending me valuable information and essays about Sasaki Kuni. In addition, Professors Nagawara and Nakagaki took the time to read the manuscript carefully and made suggestions that proved truly helpful.

I presented parts of this project in America on various occasions and received insightful comments and suggestions from a number of American scholars. I am particularly grateful to Susan Curtis for inviting me to participate in the Purdue University American Studies Symposium in April 2002, which provided me with an opportunity to present part of this book. I would also like to thank Susan Smulyan at Brown University for chairing the session at the 2002 conference of the American Studies Association in Houston where I presented a brief version of chapter 3. Her perceptive comments significantly affected the development of this chapter.

Several individuals took the time to share their knowledge with me by agreeing to be interviewed. I am extremely thankful to Junzo Nakajima, executive producer of Nippon Animation, and Akira Miyazaki, scenario writer of that studio's adaptation of *Tom Sawyer* in 1980. Mr. Miyazaki patiently and happily answered my detailed questions. Mr. Nakajima also kindly sent information on viewer ratings and generously permitted me to reprint illustrations from the film. I would also like to express my deep appreciation to Zen Enoki, president of Enoki Films, who provided me useful information about the 1994–1995 animated version of *Huckleberry Finn.* The people at Enoki Films were remarkably supportive of my research, generously lending me video recordings of this multipart series that were otherwise unavailable. I am grateful to Sachiko Kitazawa and Masaki Nishi of Enoki Films for locating these recordings and answering my miscellaneous inquiries. I would also like to thank Sakutaro Nakagawa, producer of the Twain-related television commercial for Misawa Home, and Kazuya Shigeyama, editor of the twenty-volume translation of Twain's works for Sairyusha Publishing Company, for giving their time for interviews. I am also thankful to the following people who granted me permission to reproduce material: Koji Oka, Kazunori Nagumo of Nan'-undo Publishing Co., Ltd., Tadashi Hoshino of Nippon Animation, Zen Enoki, and Hiroshi Takeuchi of Hori Production.

I owe deep gratitude to staff members at several institutions: Yasuko Doi of the International Institute for Children's Literature in Osaka, and Amy Wasserstrom, Miho Takagi, and Eiko Sakaguchi of the Gordon W. Prange Collection at the University of Maryland. I would also like to express my appreciation for the generous support of the staff members at the following research institutions: the Tsubouchi Memorial Theater Museum at Waseda University, Tokyo; the International Library of Children's Literature, Tokyo; the Research Art Center at Ritsumeikan University, Kyoto; the Textbook Library at Textbook Research Center, Tokyo; Waseda University Libarary; and Kyoto University Library. My sincere gratitude also goes to the organizations and individuals which supported my studies on Twain with the following scholarships and awards: Rotary Foundation International's Ambassadorial Scholarship; Japan–United States Educational Commission's Fulbright Grant; and the Dr. Robert Crunden Award by the Faculty of the Department of American Studies at the University of Texas at Austin.

I owe special gratitude to my wonderful friends Justin Uhr, who helped create a variety of digital images for this project, and Renata M. Fitzpatrick, who proofread the entire manuscript. Without their patience and kindness, this book would not have been possible.

My greatest debt of thanks is to my family. My parents in Japan patiently waited for my return from America and always sent me their encouragement from the other side of the globe. My sister's support was also extraordinary. She answered all my requests with great patience and sent numerous important materials with amazing speed. Her remarkable sense of humor always relieved the stress of my life in a foreign country. Finally, I would like to thank my wife, Noriko, for her encouragement, patience, and love. I could not have finished this book without her support and understanding.

Abbreviations

HB	*Huckleberry no Boken* (1948)
HF	*Adventures of Huckleberry Finn* (1885)
HFB	*Huckleberry Finn no Boken* (animated film, 1976)
HFM	*Huckleberry Finn Monogatari* (animated film, 1994–1995)
HK	"Hanamaru Kotorimaru" (1939)
HM	*Huckleberry Monogatari* (1921)
PP	*The Prince and the Pauper* (1882)
TS	*The Adventures of Tom Sawyer* (1876)
TSB	*Tom Sawyer no Boken* (animated film, 1980)
YH	*Yadonashi Huck no Boken* (1950)

Illustrations

Mark Twain in Japan

Introduction

> It seems to me that the most delightful things in "Huckleberry Finn" must disappear in a translation. One could easily translate Parkman or Emerson, certainly: but how translate Mark Twain? The only answer seems to be that if a book has vitality enough, it can live through even the brutalities of translators.
>
> Willa Cather, "A Tribute to Mark Twain"

Why are so many Japanese fascinated with one of the most distinctively American writers, Mark Twain? Over the past hundred years, Twain has influenced Japanese culture in a variety of ways. For instance, *Adventures of Huckleberry Finn* has been one of the roots of Nobel Prize–winning novelist Kenzaburo Oe's inspiration as a writer since his initial reading of the book at the age of fourteen. Oe calls *Huckleberry Finn* the work that "opened the door to the world of literature."[1] In the

1. Kenzaburo Oe, "Toni Morrison to Huckleberry Finn no Boken" (Toni Morrison and *Adventures of Huckleberry Finn*). See also Shelley Fisher Fishkin, *Lighting Out for the Territory: Reflections on Mark Twain and American Culture,* 190.

sphere of Japanese popular culture, Twain is everywhere. Twain and the characters in his works have appeared in science-fiction stories, animated television series, television commercials, musicals and other theater productions, rock music, and even a theme park. How have the Japanese assimilated Twain and his works? What kinds of alterations have they made and what were the cultural reasons behind these alterations? Are the Japanese adaptations different from American adaptations of Twain for a variety of media in American popular culture? To discuss these questions is to reveal a variety of social, historical, and cultural influences on Japanese adaptations, transformations, distortions, and rejections of the works of Mark Twain.

This book is not meant to provide a full-scale historical overview of Japanese assimilation of Twain's works. Twain's influences on Japan are too diverse for a single book to cover. Even if I restricted my focus to postwar Japanese juvenile translations of *Tom Sawyer* and *Huckleberry Finn*, there would be more than two hundred editions to discuss, making it impossible to deal with each one of them.[2] Instead, I have focused on several significant translations and adaptations and examined each in depth. I have also examined chapters of cultural history that illuminate interesting aspects of both Japan and Twain. This approach has enabled me to give the complex relationship between Twain and Japanese society and culture the attention that it deserves.

In most cases, I have chosen to discuss the Japanese versions of Twain's works that have been overlooked by scholars but that have had an important impact on the formation of the public image of Twain and his works in Japan. In keeping with the second main focus of this book, I will also discuss the ways in which both traditional and contemporary Japanese culture have transformed Twain's originals and shaped the Japanese versions. The translations and adaptations are taken up in chronological order: Taisho democracy in the 1920s (chapter 1); wartime Japan from the 1930s to 1945 (chapter 2); the postwar era from 1945 to the 1950s (chapter 3); and the 1970s through the '90s (chapter 4). The works were chosen to represent the Japanese relation-

2. The catalogue of the International Library of Children's Literature in Tokyo, the most comprehensive index of Japanese children's literature after World War II, lists 159 translations of *Tom Sawyer* and 60 of *Huckleberry Finn* between 1946 and 1995.

ship with Twain in each era. Unless otherwise indicated, all translations are mine.

The works discussed here share certain characteristics. First, they have attracted a large popular audience in Japan. Since the main concern of this book is Twain's impact on the Japanese "public" rather than on intellectuals and critics, it is necessary to pay attention to the genres that attract large audiences, such as movies and textbooks. Moreover, since Twain had been introduced to the Japanese public mainly as an author of children's literature for many decades, I also examine translations and adaptations for children. Unfortunately, many of the juvenile versions neglect Twain's complex social satire and the depth of meaning in his books. Nonetheless, these materials, which children read in their formative years, greatly affect their perception of Twain as adults. Therefore, the juvenile translations and adaptations are surely relevant to a discussion of Japanese perceptions of Twain's works.

Second, most of the works discussed here are considerably different from Twain's originals. Alterations are common among Japanese translations and adaptations aimed at popular and juvenile audiences, who are generally unfamiliar with American history and culture. However, some aspects of Twain's works have been faithfully re-created without any alterations or distortions. These retained aspects show how Twain resonates with Japanese social, cultural, and literary traditions and sensibilities, enabling audiences to assimilate his books easily. Among these "trans-U.S.-Japan" aspects of Twain's works are the didactic and genteel elements in *The Prince and the Pauper,* the small-town nostalgia in *Tom Sawyer,* and the thrilling adventure story in *Huckleberry Finn.*

This book builds on and extends the pioneering studies of two distinguished Japanese scholars, Yoshio Katsuura and Shunsuke Kamei. Katsuura's voluminous bibliographical studies, *Nihon ni okeru Mark Twain: Gaisetsu to Bunken Mokuroku* (Mark Twain in Japan: A survey and bibliography; 1979) and *Zoku Nihon ni okeru Mark Twain* (Mark Twain in Japan, continued; 1988), provide a full overview of Japanese assimilation of Twain from the 1890s to the 1980s and set an unsurpassed high standard for bibliographical studies of Twain's influences on Japan.[3] Katsuura's studies are the bible for all scholars who explore these influences, and they were valuable sources for this project as well.

However, this book differs from Katsuura's studies in two important ways. First, as already noted, I have focused on works whose main audience has been the general public rather than scholars and intellectuals. I do this because my aim is to understand public perceptions of Twain and his literature in Japan. Katsuura, especially in his second volume, was more concerned with reviewing scholarly works than examining popular and juvenile translations and adaptations. Second, this book does not attempt a bibliographical overview. Rather than replicating Katsuura's work, I have focused on selected Japanese transformations of Twain's works and how they illuminate aspects of Japanese culture and society.

Katsuura wrote another fascinating book on this theme but with a narrower focus. In *Hon'yaku no Konjaku: Mark Twain no Kotoba, Nihon-jin no Kotoba* (Translations then and now: Mark Twain's language and Japanese people's language; 1980), he examined various Japanese translations and annotated textbooks based on Twain's works. Katsuura's main concern here was the language and style of the translations and how they differ from each other. Since I am interested in the cultural impact on the translations and adaptations, I have taken a quite different approach.

In a sense, my focus is much closer to that of Shunsuke Kamei in his pioneering 1977 essay "Hikaku Bungaku: Nihon ni okeru Mark Twain" (Comparative literature: Mark Twain in Japan). Although essentially a brief overview of Twain's influences on Japan, Kamei's essay, like the present study, considered the effects of both American and Japanese cultural and literary traditions on Japanese assimilation of Twain's works. For instance, Kamei suggested that Japan's genteel literary tradition was one of the main reasons that Japanese readers appreciated *The Prince and the Pauper* earlier than Twain's other major works. He also stated that the absence of Japanese novels equivalent to *Huckleberry Finn* could be the result of "fundamental differences in cultural

3. In 1992 Katsuura published a short supplement to these books. Yoshio Katsuura, "Nihon ni okeru Mark Twain" (Mark Twain in Japan).

formations between Japan and America," including "geographical and social differences."[4] I agree with both statements.

However, just as this book differs from the work of Katsuura, it also differs from Kamei's essay in several ways. Although Kamei mainly wrote about works for adults, I examine popular culture and juvenile literature in order to understand Twain's influences on the wider Japanese public. While Kamei mainly covered the period from 1890 to 1920, I cover the period from 1920 to 2000, sketching the general trend of Twain's influences for eight decades.[5] Most importantly, Kamei's essay was too brief for him to fully examine each work's social and cultural relation with contemporary Japan. For instance, although Kamei was right when he said that the genteel literary tradition of Japan might be one of the main reasons why Japanese appreciated *The Prince and the Pauper,* he did not provide any specific examples to explain what kind of genteel literary tradition contemporary Japan had and in what way this tradition influenced Japanese appreciation of Twain's novel. In this book I provide specific examples to demonstrate the connection between Japanese versions of Twain's works and contemporary Japanese culture and society.

Several Japanese scholars have focused on Twain's influence on particular writers. For instance, there have been several studies of Takeo Arishima's short play "Domomata no Shi" (The death of Domomata; 1922), which is an adaptation of Twain's short story "Is He Living or Is He Dead?"[6] Unlike Twain's own dramatization of the story (which was

4. Shunsuke Kamei, "Hikaku Bungaku: Nihon ni okeru Mark Twain," 178, 200. In 1979, this essay was republished with slight revisions in Kamei's book *Meriken kara Amerika e: Nichibei Bunka Koshoshi Oboegaki* (From Meriken to America: Essays on cultural relations between Japan and America), 223–62.

5. In a recent essay in English, Kamei briefly discusses Twain's influences on Japan after the 1920s. Shunsuke Kamei, "Mark Twain in Japan, Reconsidered."

6. See Saburo Ota, "Mark Twain to Arishima Takeo: 'Domomata no Shi' wo meguru Mondai" (Mark Twain and Takeo Arishima: Issues around "The Death of Domomata"); Saburo Ota, "Arishima Takeo 'Domomata no Shi'" (Takeo Arishima's "The Death of Domomata"); Saeko Suzuki, "Arishima Takeo 'Domomata no Shi' no Buntai to Kosei: Mark Twain tono Kankei ni tsuite" (The style and structure of Takeo Arishima's "The Death of Domomata": On its relationship with Mark Twain); Fumiko Torii, "Arishima Takeo 'Domomata no Shi' ni tsuite" (On Takeo Arishima's "The Death of Domomata"); Yoshitaka Yoshitake, "Arishima Takeo no Hon'an-geki 'Domomata no Shi'" (Takeo Arishima's drama adaptation "The Death of Domomata").

not published until 2003),[7] the Japanese adaptation sentimentalized the original by adding a love story with a happy ending and ignoring the elements of hoax in the original, which featured the French painter François Millet as a main character. Perhaps because of Arishima's reputation as a novelist, this is the adaptation of Twain that has received the most attention from Japanese scholars. However, since his play was read only by a small group of intellectuals and students, it is beyond the scope of this book.

Few of the translations and adaptations discussed in this book have been closely examined by other scholars. For example, there has been no critical examination of Kuni Sasaki's *Huckleberry Monogatari* (The tale of Huckleberry; 1921), the first Japanese translation of *Adventures of Huckleberry Finn.* Published in various editions until the 1960s, Sasaki's version was an important model for subsequent Japanese translations of the book. Also ignored by scholars is best-selling author Jiro Osaragi's samurai novel *Hanamaru Kotorimaru* (1941), an adaptation of *The Prince and the Pauper.* Likewise, despite their impact on the public's perception of Twain, Japanese animations of *Huckleberry Finn* and *Tom Sawyer* have been almost completely overlooked except for a few brief references.[8] Although this book cannot cover all of the significant Japanese versions of Twain's works, I have explored a number of unexamined translations and adaptations as well as neglected aspects of Twain's impact on Japanese culture.[9]

7. Mark Twain, *Is He Dead? A Comedy in Three Acts.*

8. Jan B. Gordon, "Fan-Tods 'wid' de Samurai: *Huckleberry Finn* in Japan"; Toshihide Kunimatsu, "Motto Usuyogoreta Tom wo" (Waiting for a dirtier Tom Sawyer).

9. For insightful Japanese essays on Twain's influence on Japan, see Yorimasa Nasu, "Nihon ni okeru Mark Twain" (Mark Twain in Japan), and the following essays by Koutaro Nakagaki: "*Tom Sawyer* no Humor wa Ikani Inyu saretaka: Sasaki Kuni ni yoru Mark Twain no Hon'yaku" (How *Tom Sawyer*'s humor was assimilated to Japan: Kuni Sasaki's translations of Mark Twain's works); "Abekobe no Sekai: Iwaya Sazanami hoka yaku *Shonen Shosetsu Kojiki Oji* to Nichibei Jido Bungaku no Dentou" (The world of upside-down: Sazanami Iwaya and others' translations of *The Prince and the Pauper* and the tradition of U.S.-Japanese juvenile literature); and "Bungaku Kyouiku to Ideology: America Koten Jido Bungaku wo toushite saguru Nichibei Hikaku Bunka Kenkyu" (Literary education and ideology: U.S.-Japan comparative cultural studies through American juvenile classic literature). For English essays, see Shunsuke Kamei, "Mark Twain in Japan" and

One goal of this book is to show that the influence of American culture on other countries goes beyond "cultural imperialism." As several scholars have recently argued, the global influences of American culture are often too complex to be reduced to the top-down model of cultural imperialism. For example, in his study of American cultural influences on Western Europe, Richard Pells says: "Western Europe did not become a miniature version of the United States. Nor were Europeans passive victims of America's 'cultural imperialism.' Instead, the people of Western Europe adapted American culture to their own needs, tastes, and traditions, ultimately 'Europeanizing' whatever they received from the United States."[10] Of course, it would be wrong to say that the paradigm of cultural imperialism is outdated. It is persuasive enough to explain the destruction of the local cultures of countries where American cultural artifacts are mass-produced by American companies operating outside the United States. However, it is also true that the model of cultural imperialism tends to view such countries as merely passive recipients of American culture. In fact, these countries often show their autonomy by transforming, distorting, and even rejecting aspects of American culture. In his book on Tokyo Disneyland, Aviad E. Raz calls the global localization of American culture "glocalization."[11] I will use the term "Japanization" to refer to transformations and distortions of non-Japanese cultural texts and icons—Twain's texts and Mark Twain himself as a public personality—into forms suitable for a general Japanese audience. Citing examples of the Japanization of Mark Twain, this book will support Raz's view of the glocalization of American culture.

American culture does not travel only on a one-way route from

"Mark Twain in Japan, Reconsidered," and Shoji Goto, "Huck Finn and America in Kenzaburo Oe."

10. Richard Pells, *Not Like Us: How Europeans Have Loved, Hated, and Transformed American Culture since World War II,* xv. For other critical discussions on the top-down model of American cultural imperialism, see Arjun Appadurai, "Disjuncture and Difference in the Global Cultural Economy"; Uta G. Poiger, "Beyond 'Modernization' and 'Colonization'"; Heide Fehrenbach and Uta G. Poiger, eds., *Transactions, Transgressions, Transformations: American Culture in Western Europe and Japan,* xiv; Richard Kuisel, *Seducing the French: The Dilemma of Americanization,* 209; Aviad E. Raz, *Riding the Black Ship: Japan and Tokyo Disneyland,* 11–16.

11. Raz, *Riding the Black Ship,* 14, 199.

America to other countries. It is true, particularly in the sphere of popular culture, that America is almost the sole exporter of cultural products and other countries are importers. Nonetheless, cultural artifacts produced in America are often transformed in other countries and sometimes return to America to influence American culture. For instance, Japanese animation, or anime, which started under the strong influence of Disney, has gained enormous popularity in America, even influencing American animations.[12] I will demonstrate the two-way interaction of culture by discussing Japanese adaptations of Twain's works that were welcomed not only in Japan but also in America.

This book also aims to increase scholarly awareness of American cultural influences on Japan. Although a variety of perceptive studies of American cultural influences on Europe have appeared recently, studies focusing on American influences on Japanese and other Asian cultures are still rare. Considering the tremendous American cultural influence on Japan—in particular, after World War II—this scarcity of scholarship is truly surprising. There are only a few books in English that focus on American influences on Japanese popular culture, such as Taylor Atkins's *Blue Nippon: Authenticating Jazz in Japan* (2001), Aviad E. Raz's *Riding the Black Ship: Japan and Tokyo Disneyland* (1999), and Kyoko Hirano's *Mr. Smith Goes to Tokyo: Japanese Cinema under the American Occupation, 1945–1952* (1992). This scholarly neglect is reflected in the recently published anthology *"Here, There, and Everywhere": The Foreign Politics of American Popular Culture* (2000). Most of the nineteen essays in that book are about Europe and only one, an essay on Japan, focuses on an Asian country.[13] However, it would not be fair to blame the scarcity of concern with Japan on Western scholars.

12. Susan J. Napier writes that "many anime fans have seen what they believe to be heavy 'borrowing' in Disney's 1994 *Lion King* from the Tezuka Osamu classic *Kimba the White Lion.* More recently, John Lasseter, the director of the immensely popular *Toy Story* animated films, has acknowledged the influence and inspiration of the great anime director Miyazaki Hayao." Susan J. Napier, *Anime from* Akira *to* Princess Mononoke*: Experiencing Contemporary Japanese Animation,* 23. See also Yasue Kuwahara, "Japanese Culture and Popular Consciousness: Disney's *The Lion King* vs. Tezuka's *Jungle Emperor.*"

13. Reinhold Wagnleitner and Elaine Tyler May, eds., *"Here, There, and Everywhere": The Foreign Politics of American Popular Culture;* Masako Notoji, "Cultural Transformation of John Philip Sousa and Disneyland in Japan."

Even in Japan, full-scale studies of American influences on Japan in the sphere of popular culture are rare. Except for a few titles, I know of no Japanese book-length studies on this theme.[14] This book therefore explores a field neglected in both America and Japan; my hope is that it will contribute to a growing body of scholarship on the relationship between the two countries.

14. The exceptions are Takeshi Tanigawa, *Amerika Eiga to Senryo Seisaku* (American films and occupation policy; 2002); Yoshiko Takita, *American Life e no Manazashi: Shizen, Josei, Taishubunka* (Views on American life: Nature, women, and popular culture; 2000); and Kyoko Hirano, *Tenno to Seppun: America Senryoka no Nihon Eiga Ken'etsu* (Japanese emperor and kisses: The censorship of Japanese films under American occupation; 1998), which is Hirano's own translation of her book *Mr. Smith Goes to Tokyo: Japanese Cinema under the American Occupation, 1945–1952* (1992).

1

What Happened to Huck?

Kuni Sasaki's Translation of *Adventures of Huckleberry Finn*

Mark Twain was first introduced to Japan in the 1890s mainly as a writer of short stories. Translations and adaptations of his stories occasionally appeared in magazines and newspapers. Some of these were interesting and one of them caused a well-known debate between two famous translators of the time. But these early Japanese versions of Twain appeared too infrequently to arouse sustained interest among large Japanese audiences.[1]

Translations of Western literature played a significant role in the formation of modern Japanese literature. Many of the major works of Western literature were translated into Japanese in the late nineteenth century and influenced a variety of Japanese writers who were looking

1. For a list of the earliest Japanese translations of Twain's short stories, see Michiaki Kawado and Takanori Sakakibara, eds., *Mark Twain shu* (Collected works by Mark Twain), 360–62. For the debate between Hoichian Hara and Isoo Yamagata, see Kamei, "Mark Twain in Japan, Reconsidered," 75; Kamei, "Comparative Literature," 182–87; Yoshio Katsuura, *Nihon ni Okeru Mark Twain: Gaisetsu to Bunken Mokuroku* (Mark Twain in Japan: Survey and bibliography), 36–46.

for models for their own works. For instance, translations of Jules Verne's science-fiction adventure stories of the late 1800s—in particular, Shiken Morita's translation of *Deux ans de vacances* in 1896—fascinated both adult and juvenile readers and became the models for Japanese adventure stories. Shizuko Wakamatsu's colloquial translation of Frances Burnett's *Little Lord Fauntleroy* in 1891 greatly contributed to the emancipation of modern Japanese literature from traditional styles influenced by classic Chinese literature. Given the tremendous impact of Western literature and the range of translations being made available, the near neglect of Twain in Japan at the time is quite surprising.[2]

In 1898, however, the first complete translation of a major work of Twain's appeared. "Kojiki Oji" (Beggar prince), a translation of *The Prince and the Pauper,* was serialized from January through December in *Shonen Sekai* (Young boys' world), the most popular children's magazine in Japan at the turn of the century. This was a faithful translation even by today's standards, and some of the illustrations in the original American edition were carefully copied by a Japanese artist (figs. 1, 2). One year after the serialization, the translation was published in book form and acquired a wider audience. More than fifty years later, the great Japanese writer Jun'ichiro Tanizaki vividly remembered the enjoyment of reading this translation. In his memoir, Tanizaki said: "My second-favorite novel [after *New Hakkenden*] in [*Shonen Sekai*] was Beggar Prince, a translation of Mark Twain's *The Prince and the Pauper* done by Sanjin Kawa and revised by Iwaya Sazanami, with the assistance of Kuroda Kosanjin. This did not weave the strange fantasies of the *New Hakkenden,* but had rather the charm of a story that might actually have happened." In a way, this successful translation determined Twain's position in early twentieth-century Japanese popular culture. *The Prince and the Pauper* became the most popular of his works among Japanese readers until the end of World War II. It was repeatedly adapted and translated for juvenile readers by

2. See Shunsuke Kamei, "Nihon no Kindai to Hon'yaku" (The modernization of Japan and translations); Shin Torigoe, *Nihon Jido Bungaku* (Juvenile Japanese literature), 30–33; Yasuhiko Kisaichi, "Nihon no Robinsonado: Shiken-yaku Jugo Shonen no Shuhen" (Japanese Robinsonade: Issues around *Deux ans de Vacances* translated by Shiken Morita).

TOM'S MEETING WITH THE PRINCE. 39

fastened with a great sparkling gem. Several gorgeous gentlemen stood near, — his servants, without a doubt. Oh! he was a prince — a prince, a living prince, a real prince — without the shadow of a question; and the prayer of the pauper-boy's heart was answered at last.

Tom's breath came quick and short with excitement, and his eyes grew big with wonder and delight. Every thing gave way in his mind instantly to one desire: that was to get close to the prince, and have a good, devouring look at him. Before he knew what he was about, he had his face against the gate-bars. The next instant one of the soldiers snatched him rudely away, and sent him spinning among the gaping crowd of country gawks and London idlers. The soldier said, —

"Mind thy manners, thou young beggar!"

The crowd jeered and laughed; but the young prince sprang to the gate with his face flushed, and his eyes flashing with indignation, and cried out, —

"LET HIM IN!"

Fig. 1. Page 39 of Samuel L. Clemens, *The Prince and the Pauper* (Boston: James R. Osgood and Company, 1882).

フ、ツエルスの萬歳を唱へた。番兵は急かはしく鉾槍を取つて敬禮をして、直ぐに門を開けた。この貧乏國の王子が、襤褸のブラ下つて居る衣服を着て、門の中へ入る時にも、矢張り番兵は敬禮をした。そしてその場で、この貧乏國の王子であるタムと、數しれぬ富を持つて居る、英國の王子のエドワードと、親しく手を握り合つた。

「其方は大層くたびれて、腹が空いた樣に見えるが、兎も角、乃公と一同に來るがよからう。えッ、後に隨いて。エドワード、チユダーは、親切にタムを導かうとした。

その時、あちらに居た五六人の侍從たちが、あわてゝ此方へ來る樣に見えた。無論王子が此の行をいゝ止めやうと思つて來たのであらう。が、王子が手眞似で指揮したので、其まゝ來ずにそこで止まつてしまつた。やがて王子は、タムを自分の御殿の內の、立派な一室へ連れ來て、臣にいひつけて、タムにはまだ、書物でより外に見た事のない、色々な結構な食物を、あつけにとられて居るタムの前へならべさせ、なほこのあはれなお客樣が、他に見物人があ

第四卷第參號　乞食王子　(三五)

Fig. 2. The corresponding page in the Japanese translation. Sanjin Kawa et al., trans., "Kojiki Oji," *Shonen Sekai*, January 15, 1898, p. 35.

some of the country's most influential writers in the early twentieth century, such as Miekichi Suzuki and Jiro Osaragi.[3]

It seems logical that *The Prince and the Pauper,* rather than *Tom Sawyer* and *Huckleberry Finn,* was welcomed in the undemocratic social climate of imperial Japan at the turn of the century. In order to sustain a strong sense of imperial nationhood, the central government tightened the hierarchical social structure, topped by the emperor, in the late nineteenth century. In the notorious Imperial Rescript on Education, which was issued 1890 in the name of the emperor and distributed to virtually all Japanese schools, the government identified *chu* (loyalty), *ko* (filial piety), and the relationship between "benevolent rulers and their loyal subjects" as the most significant educational principles. This emphasis on loyalty to one's superiors and rulers was reflected in children's literature, and a variety of *chu-ko* stories appeared around the turn of the century.[4]

There is no doubt that the undemocratic atmosphere of imperial Japan at the turn of the century significantly shaped the Japanese reception of Twain. Japan was not yet ready for Twain's antiauthoritarian stories, such as *Tom Sawyer* and *Huckleberry Finn. The Prince and the Pauper,* on the other hand, seemed acceptable. Japanese readers were familiar not only with the royal system but also with medieval Europe through the writings of Shakespeare and Hans Christian Andersen. In addition, *The Prince and the Pauper* is, in a way, a story about the loyalty of subjects to a sovereign, which was a common theme in Japanese juvenile stories. Moreover, while the story denounces the undemocratic elements of feudalistic society, reform is made from the top to the bottom. As a result, the strict social hierarchy of royal rule remains unchanged, which was quite acceptable to imperial Japan.

However, Japan experienced a brief democratic era called Taisho

3. Sanjin Kawa, Sanjin Ko, and Sanjin Sazanami, trans., "Kojiki Oji"; Jun'ichiro Tanizaki, *Childhood Years: A Memoir,* 176–77; Miekichi Suzuki, trans., "Kojiki no Oji"; Jiro Osaragi, adapt., "Hanamaru Kotorimaru." For a stimulating essay on the 1898 translation, see Nakagaki, "The World of Upside-down." Osaragi's samurai version of *The Prince and the Pauper* is discussed in chapter 2.

4. Sazanami Iwaya's *Koganemaru* (1891), which is recognized as the first work of modern Japanese juvenile literature, was a story about a dog that is loyal to the spirits of its parents and takes revenge for its father's death with the help of loyal vassals. See also Sanmai Miyazaki, "Oya no On" (Parental love), and Gyoten Takeda, "Nidai Chuko" (Filial piety in two generations).

democracy (after Emperor Taisho) from 1918 through the 1920s. True party government finally replaced privileged government and a variety of democratic social movements, such as the women's rights movement and the movement for universal suffrage, were organized during this era. A democratic philosophy and social system were also introduced to Japan, mainly by pro-American intellectuals such as Tatsukichi Minobe, Inazo Nitobe, and Sakuzo Yoshino. These men were influential leaders of Taisho democracy and supported President Woodrow Wilson's idealistic vision of democracy.

Even in the years 1910–1930, Twain's influence on Japanese popular culture was still mainly within the sphere of children's literature, and the liberal social climate of Taisho democracy was reflected in that area as well. For instance, the Doshinshugi (Soul of Children) movement, which emphasized children's innocence and humanity, influenced Japanese children's literature of the time, emancipating juvenile stories from the tradition of loyalty and patriotism to a great degree. In this democratic cultural atmosphere, Japan was finally prepared to accept the American democratic heroes Tom Sawyer and Huck Finn.

A similar climate was evident in Germany. As a result of its defeat in World War I and the revolution of 1918, which upset its imperial regime, Germany enjoyed the brief democratic period of the Weimar Republic. Germany, too, was finally ready to welcome Tom and Huck. In 1924, Ulrich Steindorff, the translator of the new German editions of *Tom Sawyer* and *Huckleberry Finn* that appeared in the early 1920s, wrote in the *New York Times:*

> Average German adults of [the prewar] period, grounded in veneration for monarchism, were unable to appreciate the gospel of democracy; they either would or could not understand Mark Twain's smiling philosophy or his satiric mockery or his relieving laughter. And in keeping with that attitude Tom Sawyer and Huckleberry Finn, these potential free citizens of a free country, could not appeal to such parents as playmates for children. But history helped Mark Twain to enjoy the popularity prewar Germany had refused. . . . During the years 1922 and 1923 one edition of "Tom Sawyer" and "Huck Finn" followed the other, until today Mark Twain is the pet author of all German youth. About 250,000 copies now are circulating, and there is scarcely a boy or a girl to whom the two American lads are not their best playmates.[5]

5. Ulrich Steindorff, "Mark Twain's Broad German Grin: New Translations Have Helped to Restore a Lost Sense of Humor," *New York Times,* July 13, 1924.

In Japan, it was Kuni Sasaki who translated *Tom Sawyer* and *Huckleberry Finn* for the first time for his country's readers. Perhaps no individual is equal to Sasaki in his contribution to the popularity of Mark Twain in Japan. In the 1920s and '30s, Sasaki was a professor of English literature, a popular humorist, and a juvenile novelist. Above all, he was the first major translator of Mark Twain. In addition to *Tom Sawyer* and *Huckleberry Finn,* he translated *Pudd'nhead Wilson* and a number of Twain's short stories, such as "The Celebrated Jumping Frog of Calaveras County," for the first time in Japan.[6] Most of Sasaki's translations, however, were not faithful to Twain's originals. He transformed them, in accordance with the standards of Japanese juvenile literature.

Sasaki's *Tom Sawyer Monogatari* (The tale of Tom Sawyer) appeared in 1919. This was a translation for juvenile readers, and Sasaki transformed the original in two ways. First, he translated Twain's vernacular language into somewhat standard and polite Japanese. In particular, the vernacular voices of Huck and the slave Jim almost disappeared in Sasaki's grammatical Japanese. Second, as various Japanese scholars have pointed out, the love story between Tom and Becky was bowdlerized in Sasaki's *Tom Sawyer.*[7] For instance, Sasaki deleted the well-known scene in which Tom and Becky say "I love you" and exchange kisses, after which Tom reveals to Becky's dismay that she is not the first girl to whom he has been engaged. In Sasaki's version there is no engagement, no "I love you," and no kisses. Instead, Tom tries to win Becky's affection by promising that he will invite her to his circus every day when he becomes a clown.[8] Sasaki's alteration seems reasonable in light of the conservative tradition in Japanese children's literature and the differences in the custom of courtship between America and Japan. To say "I love you" is still embarrassing for most Japanese.

Although Sasaki transformed *Tom Sawyer,* his introduction of "bad

6. Kuni Sasaki, trans., "Nuke Wilson" (Pudd'nhead Wilson), "Kake Kawazu" (Gamble at frogs).

7. See Hitoshi Ishida, "Yugamerareta Tom Sawyer no Hon'yaku" (The distorted translations of *Tom Sawyer*), 44; Yoshio Katsuura, "Sasaki Kuni to Mark Twain no Sakuhin Hon'yaku" (Kuni Sasaki and his translations of Mark Twain's works), 61–62; Nakagaki, "How *Tom Sawyer*'s Humor Was Assimilated to Japan," 35–36.

8. Kuni Sasaki, *Mark Twain Meisaku Shu* (The selected works of Mark Twain), 258.

boy" figures such as Tom and Huck to contemporary Japanese children's literature was truly revolutionary. In contrast to America, which had a literary tradition of bad-boy stories, there was no equivalent tradition in Japan. Most of the boys in Japanese stories were loyal, well-tamed children without much vitality.[9] In this sense, through his *Tom Sawyer,* Sasaki opened up Japanese children's literature to fresh perspectives.

In 1921, two years after the publication of his *Tom Sawyer,* Sasaki's translation of *Adventures of Huckleberry Finn* appeared. *Huckleberry Monogatari* was published in the same juvenile translation series as the previous book. But Sasaki's Huck was even more different from Twain's original. He seemed to have forgotten many of the wonderful stories he had first told American readers thirty-six years earlier. He was changed so greatly that anyone who knew the original might have thought he was a completely different person. What had happened to Huck?

Undoubtedly, *Huckleberry Finn* was a more challenging work for both Sasaki and his readers than was *Tom Sawyer.* Huck is not a respectable boy at all; there is more violence, cruelty, and savage satire of society's hypocrisies; and most importantly, it deals with race, an issue that was seldom explored in Japanese literature. As a result, Sasaki considerably altered Twain's book, neglecting the vernacular voices, sentimentalizing Huck, insisting on Huck's respectability, neglecting Jim, and omitting Twain's satire of racism and slavery.

The vernacular voice of the protagonist has been one of the elements of *Huckleberry Finn* most highly esteemed by American scholars. In the 1930s, the influential critic Bernard DeVoto claimed that the western vernacular element of Twain's works—*Huckleberry Finn* in particular—was one of his greatest literary achievements. Leading Twain scholars in the following generations, such as Kenneth Lynn, Henry Nash Smith, and Leo Marx, shared with DeVoto their high estimation of the importance of the vernacular voices in *Huckleberry Finn.* As Shelley Fisher Fishkin demonstrated in *Was Huck Black?*

9. See Tadamichi Kan, *Nihon no Jido Bungaku* (Japanese juvenile literature), 439.

Mark Twain and African-American Voices (1993), Huck's colloquial language is still considered one of the most significant elements of *Huckleberry Finn.* True, when the book first appeared, Huck's uneducated voice was unacceptable to the genteel guardians of American literature. But *Huckleberry Finn*'s carefully crafted "unliterary" voice had a great impact on American literature in the twentieth century. We can find the influence of Huck's vernacular voice in works by such writers as Sherwood Anderson, Hemingway, Faulkner, Steinbeck, Bellow, Salinger, Ralph Ellison, and Alice Walker, to name just a few.[10]

Although it is an unimaginably difficult task to find an equivalent for Huck's American vernacular voice in Japanese, Sasaki missed its significance completely by translating it into standard Japanese. Here are the opening sentences from both Twain's original and Sasaki's translation. Twain: "You don't know about me, without you have read a book by the name of 'The Adventures of Tom Sawyer,' but that ain't no matter" (*HF,* 17). Sasaki: "'Tom Sawyer Monogatari' toiu no wo minai hito wa boku no koto wa gozonji arumai. Shikashi, sore wa boku no kono bokentan wo yomu noni nan no sashitsukae nimo naranai" (*HM,* 1). The difference between Sasaki's translation and the original is too subtle to be fully appreciated in an English retranslation. But Sasaki's Japanese is too polite and formal compared to the colloquial voice in the original. For instance, Sasaki used *gozonji* ("to know"), which is a distinctly polite Japanese expression. He ignored the colloquial rhythm of "that ain't no matter" by translating it as "sashitsukae nimo naranai," which is formal Japanese for "it does not matter." This elevation of Huck's speech is found throughout Sasaki's translation. Sasaki even omitted entire scenes depicted in Huck's vernacular voice. For instance, one of the most acclaimed passages in *Huckleberry Finn,* the description of dawn on the Mississippi that

10. Bernard DeVoto, *Mark Twain's America,* 317; Kenneth Lynn, *Mark Twain and Southwestern Humor;* Henry Nash Smith, *Mark Twain: The Development of a Writer;* Marx, *The Pilot and the Passenger: Essays on Literature, Technology, and Culture in the United States.* For a critical review of high estimations of *Huckleberry Finn* among leading Twain scholars, see Jonathan Arac, *Huckleberry Finn as Idol and Target: The Functions of Criticism in Our Time,* 154–82. For the influence of Huck's vernacular voice on twentieth-century American novelists, see Fishkin, *Lighting Out for the Territory,* 188–91.

opens chapter 19, completely disappears in Sasaki's translation.[11] Sasaki also failed to translate Jim's black dialect into equally colloquial Japanese dialect.

Although the high level of refinement of Huck's first-person vernacular speech was truly innovative when Twain published his novel in 1885, Americans were not unfamiliar with vernacular voices in literature. Mid-nineteenth-century humorists such as Artemus Ward and George Washington Harris had written stories in colloquial voices. Far West frontier vernacular had been made popular by Bret Harte's stories and Twain's "Jumping Frog." In addition, Americans were familiar with African American voices through works such as Twain's "A True Story, Repeated Word for Word as I Heard It" and Joel Chandler Harris's Uncle Remus stories. As literary realism became a pervasive trend in the late nineteenth century, readers appreciated the verisimilitude of the speech in such stories, which began to appear in mainstream literary magazines. For instance, James Russell Lowell's famous satirical verses in Yankee dialect, later published as the second series of *Biglow Papers,* appeared in the *Atlantic Monthly* during the Civil War. Parts of *Huckleberry Finn* were first published (though heavily edited) in the conservative *Century Magazine.* In contrast, when Sasaki translated *Huckleberry Finn,* Japan had no literary tradition of vernacular speech equivalent to that of America. Sasaki's neglect of the vernacular voices in *Huckleberry Finn* was largely owing to his respect for Japanese literary tradition.

Moreover, Sasaki translated *Huckleberry Finn* mainly for juvenile readers, and vernacular speech was uncommon in Japanese children's literature of the time. The Japanese Ministry of Education contributed to the tradition of formal language in children's literature and education through its strict policy of standardization of the Japanese language. In schools in the Okinawa area in the early twentieth century, for example, students who used Okinawa vernacular in class were forced to wear heavy "dialect boards" from their necks for punishment.[12]

11. For the high estimations of chapter 19 among critics, see Arac, *Huckleberry Finn as Idol and Target,* 158–75.

12. See Mikio Ando, "Dokusha no Keisei/Sakusha no Keisei" (The formation of readership/The formation of authorship), 73; Etsuo Okawa, Kin'ya Katsuo, and Mikio Ando, "Zadankai: Hogen to Jido Bungaku" (Roundtable discussion: Dialects and juvenile literature), 12.

Although some exceptional works such as Shozo Chiba's "Tora-chan Nikki" (Tora-chan's diary; 1925) employed vernacular speech, it was truly unusual, and vernacular speech was basically absent from Japanese children's literature in the early twentieth century.[13] Considering this situation, it seems reasonable to assume that Sasaki, whose literary taste was conservative compared to Twain's, either could not or would not re-create Huck's vernacular voice in equally vernacular Japanese.

The sentimentality in *Huckleberry Finn* has been neglected among scholars until relatively recently. But studies such as Leland Krauth's *Proper Mark Twain* (1999) and Gregg Camfield's *Sentimental Twain: Samuel Clemens in the Maze of Moral Philosophy* (1994) have revealed the influence of sentimental culture and philosophy on Twain and his writings. Krauth, in an essay on the connection between Victorianism and *Huckleberry Finn,* claimed that Twain rescued his novel from the unrefined tradition of southwestern humor by incorporating the sentimental literary tradition of conventional English literature.[14]

Even in light of these scholars' emphasis on sentimentality in *Huckleberry Finn,* Sasaki's sentimentalization of Huck was excessive. Sasaki's alteration of the tragic outcome of the feud between the Grangerfords and the Shepherdsons provides an example. In this scene, Huck cries over the body of Buck, his friend who was killed in the feud. Twain has Huck say, "I cried a little when I was covering up Buck's face, for he was mighty good to me" (*HF,* 155). Sasaki translated this sentence as: "I cried bitterly, dropping a lot of tears on Buck's face. He was truly kind to me. I could never forget his face in death" (*HM,* 144). The difference is considerable. Twain carefully avoided excessive sentimentality in his description. Because Huck seldom cries in the story, his deep sorrow

13. For differences and similarities between *Tom Sawyer* and "Tora-chan Nikki" and for Chiba's acknowledgment of Twain's influence on his writing, see Sho Hara, "Chiba Shozo Dowa-ron: Shozo to Twain wo Chushin ni" (An essay on Shozo Chiba's juvenile novels: Focusing on Shozo and Twain), 86–88. Chiba's condensed translation of *Tom Sawyer,* "Nishonen no Boken" (The adventures of two boys), was serialized in 1923 in his influential children's magazine *Dowa* under the pseudonym Keiji Kawamata. In 1925, under the pseudonym Taizo Souma, Chiba published "Kakebaka no Sankichi" (Sankichi, the gambling fanatic), an adaptation of "The Celebrated Jumping Frog of Calaveras County."

14. Leland Krauth, "Mark Twain: The Victorian of Southwestern Humor."

in this scene is obvious even though he simply says, "I cried a little." Sasaki's tearful translation neglects the connotations in the original and turns Huck into a more childish, sentimental character.

Sasaki even transformed Huck from a boy who hates shallow sentimentalists into a shallow sentimentalist himself. This is demonstrated by Sasaki's treatment of a scene at the Wilks mansion. The pair of frauds known as the king and the duke pretend to be the late Peter Wilks's brothers and proceed with a scheme to swindle Wilks's daughters of their father's fortune. Seeing Wilks's body in the coffin, the king and duke pretend to cry bitterly over it. Huck describes in detail the maudlin behavior of the villagers, who are easily touched by the scoundrels' fake tears. Huck concludes, "I never see anything so disgusting" (*HF,* 212). Huck is disgusted with both the behavior of the frauds and the foolish sentimentality of the villagers. Sasaki, however, had Huck say, "Even I was moved to tears" (*HM,* 193). Disregarding Twain's portrayal of Huck as a realistic boy with a doubtful mind, Sasaki transformed him into an uncritical sentimentalist.

There seems to be some connection between Sasaki's sentimentalization of Huck and contemporary trends in Japanese juvenile literature. As several scholars have pointed out, realistic boys with vitality and critical minds are rare in this literature.[15] Tadamichi Kan, Japan's leading scholar of juvenile literature, suggests that characters like Huck and Tom are absent even in realistic novels of Japanese children's literature:

> The images of children such as Tom Sawyer and Huckleberry Finn were not created by so-called Actual-life or Realist children's story schools [in Japan]. Tom or Huck's defiant behaviors were based upon their vitality and severely critical minds, which would trouble the moral guardians of churches and schools. In other words, their disobedient

15. See Mikio Ando et al., "Mark Twain kara Nani wo Uketsugu ka" (What do we learn from Mark Twain), 33–38; Ando, "Formation of Readership," 59; Mikio Ando, "Kindai Nihon Jido Bungaku no Houhou to Ningen-zou" (The methods and images of characters in modern Japanese juvenile literature), 202; Teruo Jingu, "Sekai-teki Shiya no Naka deno Jido Bungaku" (Juvenile literature from a global perspective), 22; Tadao Sato, "Shonen no Riso-shugi" (The idealism of boys), 134; Shin Torigoe, "Boken Shosetsu no Miseijuku: Kaku Realism no Kanosei" (Immaturity of adventure novels: A possibility of fantastic realism), 222.

> behaviors were the result of their challenges to the hypocrisy, formalism, and corruption of adult society, which caused problematic situations among children. It is reasonable to say that, in the tradition of Japanese children's literature, almost no work depicted realistic images of bad boys which reflect those problematic situations.[16]

In particular, early twentieth-century Doshinshugi juvenile literature, which was very influential when Sasaki's *Huck* appeared, often disregarded the real attributes of children as a result of its idealization of their innocence. Takashi Kan stated the problem as follows: "As a result of its emphasis on idealistic images of children, [Taisho Doshinshugi literature] was inclined toward abstract notions of humanism (and sometimes mere sentimentalism), neglecting children's egos and bodies."[17] Although Sasaki's sentimental Huck often shows more "pluck" compared to the delicate boys in Doshinshugi literature, it is also true that Sasaki transformed Huck to accommodate him to the somewhat sentimental literary climate of the time.

When Twain wrote *Tom Sawyer* and *Huckleberry Finn,* there was already a literary genre of the so-called bad boy's story in America. Thomas Bailey Aldrich, who became a friend of Twain, had published his influential autobiographical novel *The Story of a Bad Boy* in 1870 and started the emancipation of American children's literature from the shackles of its literary tradition of didacticism. After the success of Aldrich's book, a variety of similar stories appeared in America, including Charles Dudley Warner's *Being a Boy* (1878), Benjamin P. Shillaber's *Ike Partington and His Friends* (1879), Metta V. F. Victor's *A Bad Boy's Diary* (1880), George W. Peck's *Peck's Bad Boy and His Pa* (1883), William Dean Howells's *A Boy's Town* (1890), and Edward Eggleston's *The Hoosier Schoolmaster* (1893). Although critics have suggested that Tom Sawyer and Huck Finn were different from these tamed and sometimes devilish bad-boy figures in many ways,[18] the fact remains that

16. Kan, *Japanese Juvenile Literature,* 439.

17. Takashi Kan, afterword to *Jido Bungaku to Shakai: Houkoku to Shinpojiumu* (Juvenile literature and society: Report and symposium), 228.

18. See Albert E. Stone, *The Innocent Eye: Childhood in Mark Twain's Imagination,* 31, 72, 266; Anne Scott MacLeod, *American Childhood: Essays on Children's Literature,* 71.

American readers were ready to accept bad-boy stories in the late nineteenth century and Twain benefited from this liberal climate.

Japan, however, did not have an equivalent literary tradition of bad-boy stories. Even today, we can hardly find in Japanese children's literature a character like Huck who smokes, swears, and steals. Japanese critics and writers agree that the didactic literary climate is one of the reasons for the absence of bad boys. Here is a conversation among Yuhi Takezaki, Mikio Ando, Yasue Miyagawa, and Masako Shimizu, leading critics and writers of children's literature:

Takezaki:	Well, in the end, it's a question of whether we can let the children smoke in our novels.
Ando:	I think we should let them if we need to.
Takezaki:	Of course, it is okay to let them, but the question is, can we really accept it?
Ando:	Well, that's right. [Snicker] Very didactic, our literature is.
Miyagawa:	Writers are good students, too.
Shimizu:	Right. That's why we don't have Mark Twain and Tom Sawyer.[19]

Without a literary tradition of bad-boy stories to rely upon, Sasaki made *Huckleberry Finn* genteel for his juvenile readers by complying with the respectable literary norm.

Sasaki's Huck is also more respectable and educated than Twain's. He does not steal. He has even memorized the multiplication table, correctly saying that "seven times seven is forty-nine" (*HM,* 13); Twain's Huck says that "six times seven is thirty-five" (*HF,* 34). More significantly, Sasaki altered the famous scene in chapter 31 in which Huck decides to help Jim, who has been captured, even if it means he will "go to hell." In this scene, Huck writes a letter to Jim's rightful owner and tells her where Jim is. Looking at the letter, Huck has warm memories of Jim and their journey on the raft and realizes how kind and caring Jim has been to him. Torn between the rule of a slaveholding society and his friendship with Jim, Huck struggles over whether to send the letter and turn Jim in or help rescue him instead.

19. Ando et al., "What Do We Learn from Mark Twain," 35. See also Jingu, "Juvenile Literature from a Global Perspective," 27.

> It was a close place. I took [the letter] up, and held it in my hand. I was a-trembling, because I'd got to decide, forever, betwixt two things, and I knowed it. I studied a minute, sort of holding my breath, and then says to myself:
>
> "All right, then, I'll *go* to hell"—and tore it up.
>
> It was awful thoughts, and awful words, but they was said. And I let them stay said; and never thought no more about reforming. I shoved the whole thing out of my head; and said I would take up wickedness again, which was in my line, being brung up to it, and the other warn't. And for a starter, I would go to work and steal Jim out of slavery again; and if I could think up anything worse, I would do that, too; because as long as I was in, and in for good, I might as well go the whole hog. (*HF*, 272)

Sasaki translated the passage as follows:

> I took [the letter] up and read it, then I says trembling: "All right. I'll go to hell for Jim. I'll accept this trouble, for I want to be a good boy"—and tore it up. [The following paragraph was omitted.] (*HM,* 274–75)

What happened to Huck's crucial decision to become a wicked boy to help Jim? Where is Twain's bitterly ironic critique of the slaveholding society where to become wicked is the only way to do the right thing? By turning *Huckleberry Finn* into a mere "good-boy story," Sasaki made it acceptable as a Japanese children's book, but he considerably distorted Twain's ironic art.

Huck is not the only character who was transformed. Sasaki's neglect of Jim was perhaps his widest divergence from Twain's intentions. Many significant scenes in the original book that show Jim's dignity and humanity were deleted in Sasaki's translation. A famous scene in chapter 15 is one example. One night, Huck, in a canoe, and Jim, on the raft, are separated from each other by the swift current and dense fog of the Mississippi. Although they do their best to find each other, they fail. When Huck finally finds the raft in the morning, Jim is asleep, having worn himself out in his struggle to find Huck. Huck wakes Jim up and plays a trick on him by insisting they have been together on the raft for the whole night. He persuades Jim that the fog and their separation must have been a dream, and he encourages Jim to tell him about it. It is not until Jim comes to the end of his story, which he has embellished with exaggerated terrors, that he realizes he has been fooled by Huck. Jim shames Huck by contrasting his own concern for Huck's life with Huck's plan to make a fool of him. Although it was most unusual for a white to apologize to a black in a slaveholding society, Huck humbles himself and sincerely apologizes to Jim (*HF*, 115–21). This scene is crucial since it shows Huck, perhaps for the first time, learning that even a slave can be bitterly hurt when his friendship and dignity are trampled upon. This is the moment when Huck demonstrates that Jim has become so important to him that he will even sacrifice his pride as a white to maintain their friendship. However, this significant scene is completely omitted in Sasaki's translation.

Sasaki also omitted the aspect of Jim as a caring father who deeply loves his family. In chapter 16, Huck describes what Jim plans to do after his escape to a free state. Twain's Huck says: "He was saying how the first thing he would do when he got to a free State he would go to saving up money and never spend a single cent, and when he got enough he would buy his wife, which was owned on a farm close to where Miss Watson lived; and then they would both work to buy the two children, and if their master wouldn't sell them, they'd get an Ab'litionist to go and steal them" (*HF*, 123–24). In Sasaki's translation, Huck says: "Jim said that when he got to a free State he would go to saving up money and never spend a single cent, and buy his wife. He also said that he'd like to buy rice paddies and two children or so. He was in a happy mood building some other castles in the air suitable for a nigger" (*HM*, 107). Sasaki's mistranslation is obvious. Although Jim is planning to buy his *own* two children in order to emancipate them from slavery, Sasaki has him planning to buy two random children as if he, like the slaveowners, saw them as commodities. Twain's Jim loves his family so dearly that he even thinks of asking the help of an abolitionist to get them back. Sasaki deleted this part of the plan, which shows Jim's love toward his children.

Jim's deep affection for his family is never shown more emotionally than when Twain has Huck overhear him mournfully saying, "Po' little 'Lizabeth! po' little Johnny! its mighty hard: I spec' I ain't gwyne to see you no mo', no mo'!" Huck explains: "He was thinking about his wife and his children, away up yonder, and he was low and homesick; . . . and I do believe he cared just as much for his people as white folks does for their'n. It don't seem natural, but I reckon it's so" (*HF,* 201). Again, Sasaki deleted this scene. The result of such deletions is that Sasaki failed to introduce Jim as a caring father who has both family and dignity, turning him into a merely obedient and somewhat foolish character.

Sasaki's distortions of Jim seem to reflect Japanese people's deep-seated prejudices against blacks at the time. It was not black America but white America that Japan had recognized as its model since its encounter with America in the mid-nineteenth century. As a result, the Japanese assimilated white American racism toward blacks. Masao Miyoshi, the leading scholar of the cultural relationship between the two countries, says: "In their identification with the white Americans, they were prepared to reject any people the white Americans scorned. Thus American racism did not bother them much, nor did white supremacy, since the Japanese would be like the whites some day." Miyoshi describes the racist views among samurai officers who went on the first official Japanese mission to America in 1860. One samurai wrote: "The blacks are inferior as human beings and extremely stupid. They are segregated from the whites, and no blacks are wealthy." Another wrote: "They are just like our *eta* caste [the lowest class of paupers]. . . . The whites are of course intelligent, and the blacks stupid." Even in the early twentieth century, some Japanese intellectuals looked down on African American culture, such as jazz, calling it "a culture of barbarism."[20] In Japanese children's literature, racist views sometimes appeared in colonialist adventure stories. In Oshikawa Shunro's *Shin Nihon-jima* (New Japanese island), a 1906 best-seller about the Japanese colonization of Africa, for instance, the native blacks are portrayed as foolish characters who obediently follow the orders of the Japanese. Similar images of blacks continued to appear in Japanese juvenile stories up until World War II. In *Boken Dankichi* (Adventures of Dankichi), a popular comic strip serial in Japanese juvenile magazines in the 1930s, a Japanese boy becomes king of an island of blacks and

20. Masao Miyoshi, *As We Saw Them: The First Japanese Embassy to the United States,* 64, 61; Kamei, *From Meriken to America,* 92.

dehumanizes his subjects by painting identification numbers on their bodies.[21] Even though Sasaki had a more liberal and democratic mindset than most of his contemporaries, he probably shared some of their prejudices against blacks and therefore minimized the importance of Jim in *Huckleberry Finn.*

Sasaki also tended to disregard Twain's satirical attacks on racism and slavery. He altered or deleted Twain's most vivid depictions of racism in the slaveholding South. For instance, Pap Finn's famous "free nigger" speech was completely eliminated from Sasaki's translation. In this speech, Huck's drunkard father vents his anger against the "gov'-ment" for giving voting rights to a free mulatto professor from Ohio. He condemns the government for allowing the mulatto to have a respectable life, contrasting it with his own miserable life of poverty (*HF,* 49–50). Pap's speech vividly shows the way in which poor whites sought solace by discriminating against the underclass, the blacks. Although the situation was different, Japan had a similar problem of discrimination against an underclass. The "buraku kaiho undo," the emancipation movement of the underclass, became very active in the era of Taisho democracy when Sasaki translated *Huckleberry Finn.* Minorities such as Korean and Chinese residents were also discriminated against in a variety of ways in Japanese society. However, failing to recognize the significance of *Huckleberry Finn,* a book that could shed light on these serious issues, Sasaki turned it into an innocuous juvenile story.

Sasaki also changed the meaning of one of the bitterest examples of Twain's social satire, the brief exchange between Huck and Aunt Sally in chapter 32. This episode shows that even the affectionate Aunt Sally accepts the racist definition of *person* that was common in the slaveholding society. On hearing of a steamboat accident, Sally says, "Good gracious! Anybody hurt?" Huck answers, "No'm. Killed a nigger," and Sally responds, "Well, it's lucky; because sometimes people do get hurt" (*HF,* 280). In Sasaki's translation, Sally expresses sympathy for the dead black, saying, "Oh, my!" (*HM,* 287). Her comment "sometimes

21. Keizo Shimada, *Boken Dankichi Manga Zenshu* (*Boken Dankichi* comic strip collection). See also John G. Russell, *Nihonjin no Kokujin-kan* (Japanese images of blacks), 87.

people do get hurt" is omitted. In elevating the character of Aunt Sally and revising her racist view, Sasaki sacrificed Twain's bitter satire of the racism of a slaveholding society. Sasaki's sugarcoated translation of *Huckleberry Finn* might have been suitable for the innocent juvenile Japanese readers of the time, but it is not the *Huckleberry Finn* Twain wrote.

Twain's art of irony often lost its power in Sasaki's translation. Twain's criticisms of slavery and racism are not straightforward most of the time; irony was one of his most powerful weapons in attacking social injustice. As Twain later wrote in his notebook, *Huckleberry Finn* is a story about a struggle between a boy's "sound heart" and his "deformed conscience."[22] To help a runaway slave was considered one of the greatest sins in a slaveholding society. As a white boy growing up in the antebellum South, Huck is perhaps more familiar with this rule than with any other. His conscience is based on this fundamental rule of slaveholding society. Huck is torn between following his "sound heart" and helping Jim escape from slavery or following the social rule and turning Jim in. The irony of this struggle touches readers, since they know that Huck is doing the right thing to help Jim escape. At the same time, the struggle artfully reveals the social injustices of slavery that continuously torture Huck's "sound heart."

In chapter 16, there is a significant moment when Huck's "deformed conscience" is tested. Horrified at hearing Jim's plan to buy or steal his family from their owners, Huck finally decides to turn Jim in. He takes a canoe to the shore to report Jim as a runaway slave. Two slave hunters approach and ask Huck whether the person on his distant raft is black or white. This is Huck's best chance to turn Jim in. If he answers "black," that's the end of the story. Huck hesitates, then finally says, "He's white" (*HF,* 124). This scene is omitted from Sasaki's translation.

The climax of Huck's struggle is perhaps the moment when he decides to "go to hell" to help Jim. As we have seen, Sasaki considerably altered Huck's words here, turning him into a mere "good boy." But Sasaki's distortion was not limited to Huck's remarks. Right before this

22. Twain's journal entry of August 23, 1895, quoted in Walter Blair, *Mark Twain and Huck Finn,* 143.

climactic scene, Twain depicted Huck's inner struggle in detail, and in this way intensified the seriousness of his final decision to help Jim:

> I most dropped in my tracks I was so scared. Well, I tried the best I could to kinder soften it up somehow for myself by saying I was brung up wicked, and so I warn't so much to blame; but something inside of me kept saying, "There was the Sunday-school, you could a gone to it; and if you'd a done it they'd a learnt you there that people that acts as I'd been acting about that nigger goes to everlasting fire."
>
> It made me shiver. . . . You can't pray a lie—I found that out. (*HF*, 270)

However, Sasaki's Huck simply says, "The more I thought about this problem the harder it got, and I could not find the way to get out of it" (*HM*, 273). Twain's Huck has a profound fear of punishment by God, based on his innocent belief in a Calvinistic executor of fearful punishments such as burning sinners alive in "everlasting fire." He literally believes in hell. That is the reason why his decision to "go to hell" to help Jim is the most serious decision he can make. By ignoring Huck's innocent but very serious inner struggle, Sasaki considerably weakened the significance of his decision to "go to hell." At the same time, Sasaki lost one of the best chances to show that slavery was founded upon the hypocrisy of respected social institutions such as church and Sunday school, and that Huck's decision is an open revolt against the rules of the established social system. As a result, Sasaki's *Huck* lost the satirical power of Twain's original, a book that challenges the foundations of society through irony.

Although it is impossible to fully explain his decisions, Sasaki's neglect of Twain's satire of slavery and racism seems reasonable in light of the social differences between Japan and the United States. Perhaps Sasaki bowdlerized the provocative elements of the original so that his translation would conform to the genteel norm of early twentieth-century Japanese juvenile literature, which seldom employed satire and irony for social criticism. In this case, however, the difference between Japanese and American perceptions of racism is still significant. As we have seen, Japan has never been free from prejudices against minorities. In this sense, *Huckleberry Finn* has the potential to to provoke Japanese readers to ponder the problems of discrimination in their own country. However, in most cases, prejudices against minorities in Japan are based on ethnicity rather than color. It is true that Japan has a long history of racism, as evidenced by its discrimination against the Ainu people. Moreover, as John Dower revealed in his pathbreaking study *War without Mercy,* the Japanese had severely racist views toward whites, particularly during World War II. Until recently, however, when Japan became a more racially diverse society, racism was not considered as serious an issue as Japanese discrimination toward East Asians, particularly Korean and Chinese residents, whose skin color is the same as that of the majority of Japanese. Unlike many Americans, who lived in a racially diverse society, early twentieth-century Japanese were not in a position to develop sensitivity about issues of race.[23] Considering the unfamiliarity of racial issues in early twentieth-century Japan, it is highly probable that Sasaki deleted or weakened Twain's attacks on racism and slavery in deference to the Japanese public, particularly juvenile readers.

While it is important to pay close attention to Sasaki's "transformations" of *Huckleberry Finn,* it is equally important to examine the parts of the book he faithfully re-created, since these parts contain the images that Sasaki clearly chose to emphasize. The last twelve chapters, known as the "evasion" episode, make up the section that Sasaki translated most faithfully. There were almost no distortions and omissions. Although Twain devoted only 89 pages to this episode, equal to less than a quarter (24.3 percent) of the book, Sasaki gave it 150 pages, equivalent to more than one-third (35.6 percent) of his translation. (The Japanese translation had fewer lines per page than the original.) In a way, this figure shows how faithful Sasaki's translation of this section is in comparison with the rest of the story, which he shortened considerably.

However, considering the variety of poor responses it has received in America, Sasaki's faithfulness to the ending of *Huckleberry Finn* seems rather unusual. Echoing Hemingway's famous suggestion to ig-

23. For the development of Japanese people's awareness about their racism in the late twentieth century, particularly against blacks, see my discussion in chapter 4, pp. 98, 113.

nore the ending altogether, a number of American adaptations and revised editions of *Huckleberry Finn* have transformed or eliminated the "evasion" episode. For instance, Charles Neider's revised edition of *Huckleberry Finn,* published in 1985, condensed or deleted the final chapters. John Seelye completely eliminated the episode in his adaptation, *The True Adventures of Huckleberry Finn* (1970; revised in 1987). Many of the film adaptations of *Huckleberry Finn* have followed this trend as well.[24]

As many critics have pointed out, the main reason for these negative responses to the ending is the reappearance of Tom Sawyer and the dominance he assumes over the story.[25] Concealing the fact that Jim has been freed by his owner, Tom contrives to have him imprisoned in a shack and then hatches an elaborate scheme to release him from captivity. Following Tom's instructions, Jim performs a variety of unnecessary tasks in preparation for the escape. In these last chapters, both Huck and Jim are reduced to reluctant participants in Tom's childish scheme. Tom injures Jim's dignity just for the sake of his fun, and Jim seldom refuses his foolish commands. Huck is also belittled. Although Huck has learned to see Jim as a person, not as a slave, and developed a true friendship with him, he is too impressed with Tom to do anything other than follow along. Moreover, Huck's crucial decision to "go to hell" to help Jim turns out to be somewhat farcical, since Jim has already been freed in his deceased owner's will.

In Sasaki's translation the ending does not seem as contradictory as it does in the original. In the translation, as we have seen, both Jim's dignity and Huck's inner struggle have been minimized even before Tom's reappearance. As a result, the ending does not seem inconsistent with the rest of the story. In a sense, Sasaki was Tom's accomplice in his treatment of Huck and Jim, and that is why the ending, dominated by Tom, fits Sasaki's *Huckleberry Finn* perfectly.

24. Ernest Hemingway, *Green Hills of Africa,* 22; Charles Neider, ed., *Adventures of Huckleberry Finn;* John Seelye, *The True Adventures of Huckleberry Finn.* For film adaptations, see *The Adventures of Huckleberry Finn,* dir. Richard Thorpe, MGM, 1939; *Adventures of Huckleberry Finn,* dir. Peter H. Hunt, Great Amwell/PBS, 1985; *The Adventures of Huck Finn,* dir. Stephen Sommers, Disney, 1993.

25. See, for example, Smith, *Mark Twain: The Development of a Writer,* 133–34; Leo Marx, "Mr. Eliot, Mr. Trilling, and Huckleberry Finn."

Sasaki's faithful translation of the ending shows the essence of his views on *Huckleberry Finn.* As we have seen, Sasaki considerably weakened Twain's social criticisms, eliminating or transforming his satire. The ending seems suitable for this innocuous *Huckleberry Finn,* a juvenile story with no severe social criticism. In the original book, Huck's ironic struggle with the norms of his slaveholding society are largely replaced by his detailed and lengthy depiction of Tom's childish scheme. As a result, the ending seems to considerably weaken the social criticism in other parts of the novel. This was very convenient for Sasaki's uncritical *Huckleberry Finn.* As shown by his untiringly faithful translation of the details of Tom's elaborate scheme, Sasaki apparently welcomed Tom's dominance of the final chapters. Perhaps what Sasaki wanted to see in Huck was another Tom Sawyer, a childish romantic who can easily avoid facing the injustices of hypocritical society, rather than a realist who ironically cannot help facing them. In this sense, Tom Sawyer was a savior for Sasaki, rescuing his *Huckleberry Finn* from Twain's dangerous world of satire and social criticism.

Sasaki attributed his career as a humorist to the influence of Mark Twain, and we can find traces of Twain in Sasaki's own novels, which were popular in Japan in the 1920s and '30s. For instance, in his earliest fiction, *Chintaro Nikki* (Chintaro's diary; 1920), Sasaki included a humorous sketch about ants from one of Twain's European travelogues without mentioning its source.[26] Moreover, in one of his juvenile stories, *Mura no Shonen-dan* (Boy scouts in a village; 1930–1932), Sasaki wrote episodes that are similar to those in *Tom Sawyer,* such as a treasure hunt, an adventure in a haunted mansion, and a violent criminal character reminiscent of Injun Joe.

However, as a whole, Sasaki's novels about boys are very different from *Tom Sawyer* and *Huckleberry Finn.* Although some of the boys in his novels occasionally turn a critical eye toward adult society, most of them are well-behaved compared to Tom and Huck. They are obedient to their teachers, use polite language, and even care about their grades.

26. Kuni Sasaki, "Kokusai Mark Twain Kyokai" (The International Association for Mark Twain), 346–47. For the sketch about ants, see Kuni Sasaki, *Chintaro Nikki,* 256; for the original, see Twain, *A Tramp Abroad,* 215–19.

Moreover, in Sasaki's novels, it is hard to find social satire as severe and challenging as that found in *Huckleberry Finn.* Neither can we find a serious revolt against society, such as Huck's decision to "go to hell." Though Sasaki was named an honorary member of the Mark Twain Society of America in the 1950s, it does not seem right to call him the "Japanese Mark Twain" based on his novels.[27]

Nevertheless, it is also true that Twain, through Sasaki, contributed to the development of modern Japanese popular literature. Sasaki, a pioneer of humor in modern Japan, enriched its literature, which was notorious for its lack of humor.[28] Moreover, Sasaki shared Twain's anti-nationalistic and anti-imperialistic sentiments. Although he did not criticize government policy as straightforwardly as Twain did, Sasaki was one of the rare popular writers who never accommodated to the militaristic and imperialistic sentiment in Japan from the 1930s to the end of World War II. He was never part of the anti-American social climate based on the militaristic ultranationalism of Japan at the time. He even wrote a novel called *Tomu-kun Samu-kun* (Tom-boy and

27. Sasaki, "Kokusai Mark Twain Kyokai," 346–47. Taro, the narrator of *Itazura Kozo Nikki* (A bad boy's diary; 1901), is probably Sasaki's most mischievous bad-boy character. However, although scholars and critics long believed that *Itazura Kozo Nikki* is Sasaki's fiction, it has been shown that it is in fact a liberal translation of an anonymous American novel, *A Bad Boy's Diary* (1880). Isao Horibe, "*Itazura Kozo Nikki* no Gensho" (The original text of *Itazura Kozo Nikki*); Yasuo Nishizaki, "Sasaki Kuni no Jido Bungaku: *Itazura Kozo Nikki* Kenkyu" (Kuni Sasaki's juvenile literature: A study of *Itazura Kozo Nikki*), 53–56. The author of this anonymous novel was Metta Victoria Fuller Victor, a female American dime novelist, and Sasaki's succeeding "bad boy" and "bad girl" novels were adaptations of her other anonymous novels. In short, Sasaki did not create his own "bad boy" and "bad girl" characters. See Tsuyoshi Ishihara, "Sasaki Kuni to Metta Victoria Fuller Victor." Twain detested *A Bad Boy's Diary,* saying, "I would not be the author of that witless stuff for a million dollars." Samuel Clemens to Charles L. Webster, September 19, 1882, in Samuel Charles Webster, ed., *Mark Twain, Business Man,* 197.

28. Joel R. Cohn calls Sasaki, who started the literary magazine *Humor Club* in 1937, one of the significant figures who challenged the "cult of seriousness" of naturalism and Shishosetsu (the autobiographical novel) that dominated Japanese literature in the 1920s and '30s. Joel R. Cohn, *Studies in the Comic Spirit in Modern Japanese Fiction,* 30. For the lack of humor in modern Japanese literature, see Kunio Yanagita, "Warai no Bungaku no Kigen" (The origin of literature of humor); Mitsuo Nakamura, "Warai no Soshitsu" (Disappearance of humor), 113–15; Cohn, *Studies in the Comic Spirit,* 187.

Sam-boy) in 1933 that obviously criticized these superficial sentiments by celebrating the friendship between an American boy and a Japanese boy. This was at a time when anti-American stories were becoming popular in children's magazines. During World War II, Sasaki kept his silence.[29] Considering that the oppressive wartime government arrested and even executed intellectuals who voiced antigovernment opinions, Sasaki's silent resistance should not be underestimated. During this time, Twain's democratic and antiauthoritarian elements were still alive in Sasaki's books.

Sasaki's *Huckleberry Monogatari* was read widely among the Japanese public, particularly juvenile readers, after its appearance in 1921. In 1932, eleven years after its first publication, it was reprinted by another company and acquired an even larger readership. In Japan, it was the only translation of *Huckleberry Finn* for twenty years, until Tameji Nakamura's more faithful translation for adult readers was published in 1941. Even after several new Japanese translations of *Huckleberry Finn* appeared after World War II, Sasaki's translation was reprinted a number of times for juvenile readers by major publishing companies, going through several impressions until the early 1960s. Sasaki's *Huck* therefore influenced Japanese understanding of *Huckleberry Finn* for forty years.

As we have seen, Sasaki failed to fully re-create Twain's masterpiece, neglecting or distorting significant scenes. Even so, *Huckleberry Finn* was a revolutionary book in the world of Japanese juvenile literature. In that genteel climate, a juvenile-delinquent hero such as Huck was very unusual. Even in Sasaki's bowdlerized translation, Huck still smokes, "plays hooky," and swears. Furthermore, it would not be fair to blame Sasaki for the distortions in his translation while ignoring the considerable cultural differences between Japan and America in the early twentieth century. Twain's works, particularly *Huckleberry Finn,* were literally created from American culture: American humor, southwestern vernacular, the tradition of bad-boy stories, African American voices, the natural beauty of the Mississippi, American frontier villages, and

29. Sumi Kosakai, *Hyoden Sasaki Kuni: Humor Sakka no Ganso Koko ni Ari* (Kuni Sasaki, a Biography: Here is the father of Japanese humorists), 165–66.

so on. Early twentieth-century Japan was unfamiliar with these elements of American culture. In Japan there was no equivalent to the Mississippi, almost no frontier villages, little chance to interact with African Americans, no literary tradition of bad-boy stories or vernacular speech, and little use of humor in literature. In light of these cultural differences, Sasaki's transformations might have been unavoidable if *Huckleberry Finn* was to become a part of Japanese culture. In addition, Sasaki translated *Huckleberry Finn* not for scholars or critics upon whose refined knowledge he could rely, but for the general public—in particular, juvenile readers whose knowledge about American culture and society was very limited. In order to satisfy these readers, Sasaki needed to cater to their tastes. Finally, *Huckleberry Finn* is undoubtedly one of the most challenging works for translators, mainly for its "untranslatable" American vernacular voices. Considering all these difficulties, we should hold Sasaki's first Japanese translation of *Huckleberry Finn* in high esteem as a pioneer work for succeeding generations.

2

Mark Twain in Wartime Japan

The Samurai Version of *The Prince and the Pauper*

The period from the 1930s to the end of World War II was undoubtedly the most problematic era in the history of the Japanese reception of Mark Twain's works. It was a time when ultranationalism, militarism, and anti-Americanism intensified in Japan. Right-wing politicians and army officers seized control of the country, setting Japan on a course of militarist expansionism in Asia. The United States–Japan relationship deteriorated, largely as a result of the Anti-Japanese Immigration Act in 1924 and the Japanese invasion of China in the 1930s. As a result, an anti-American climate became dominant. Many of the pro-American liberal intellectuals of Taisho democracy died in the 1930s, and the few that remained were severely oppressed by the militaristic government. Pro-American intellectual leaders Sakuzo Yoshino and Inazo Nitobe both died in 1933. Tatsukichi Minobe, who claimed there were legal limitations to the emperor's power, was forced to resign from the Japanese Diet in 1935 and his books were suppressed by the government. American popular culture was also suppressed from the late 1930s to the end of the war. In 1938, for instance, the government set a limit on the number of American films that could be imported to Japan. Even American elements in Japanese popular culture were censored by the government. For instance, Akira Kurosawa was forced to delete the birthday party scene in his wartime screenplay *San-pugita no Hana* (The San Pugita flowers) and the "so-called love scene" in his film *Sanshiro Sugata* (1943), about the famous judo wrestler, because the censorship bureau considered them "Anglo-American."[1] During the war English became taboo, and even baseball terms were translated into awkward Japanese.

The nationalistic cultural climate was also reflected in Japanese popular and juvenile literature, the sphere in which Twain was introduced to the public. In the 1930s, Japanese writers tended to take traditional Japanese materials rather than foreign materials for their subjects. In the sphere of Japanese popular and juvenile literature, the 1930s was the golden age of "magemono" novels, samurai stories situated in feudal Japan. A number of samurai novels, such as Eiji Yoshikawa's *Miyamoto Musashi* and Jiro Osaragi's *Kurama Tengu,* were serialized in Japanese newspapers, magazines, and juvenile magazines and acquired tremendous popularity. The samurai heroes in these stories soon became national heroes through numerous radio and film adaptations.

Amid this boom of samurai stories, "Hanamaru Kotorimaru," a samurai version of *The Prince and the Pauper,* appeared. The author of this adaptation was Jiro Osaragi, one of the representative magemono writers of the time. The novel was serialized in *Shonen Kurabu* (Boy's club), the country's most popular juvenile magazine, in twelve monthly installments in 1939. As we have seen, in 1898 *The Prince and the Pauper* was the first major work of Twain's to be introduced to Japan, and it was perhaps the most popular of Twain's works in that country until the end of World War II. By 1939 it had already been translated into Japanese four times—more than any other major work by Twain. In fact, "Hanamaru Kotorimaru" was not even the first Japanese version of *The Prince and the Pauper* to appear in *Shonen Kurabu.* In 1930

1. Kyoko Hirano, *Mr. Smith Goes to Tokyo: Japanese Cinema under the American Occupation, 1945–1952,* 25, 21.

the magazine serialized Seijiro Kojima's relatively faithful Japanese translation of *The Prince and the Pauper,* "Kojiki Oji."[2]

However, in the ultranationalistic cultural atmosphere of the late 1930s, a samurai version of *The Prince and the Pauper* was surely more welcome than a faithful translation. The editorial tendency of *Shonen Kurabu* vividly reflects this atmosphere. As anti-British and anti-American sentiments intensified, translations of English and American literature virtually disappeared from the pages of the magazine. At the same time, nationalistic and militaristic stories about imagined United States–Japan wars and idealized Japanese war heroes appeared frequently.[3]

In 1939, a number of nationalistic war stories, pro-German essays, and anti-British and anti-American essays appeared along with "Hanamaru Kotorimaru" in *Shonen Kurabu.* One essay celebrated Hitler's invasion of Czechoslovakia. In a story called "Nihon e no Hakushu" (Applause to Japan), a Japanese boy who lives in California protects his Chinese friend from the bullying of racist American students. This story was clearly an attempt to justify the Japanese invasion of Asia by portraying Japan in the role of protector of weak Asian countries from Western attacks. In addition, in an announcement of the Magazine Week movement of 1939, the editors of the magazine betrayed their fanatic militaristic nationalism:

> It has been said that the "magazine is the bullets of the heart which are necessary for both the front and the home front during the war." We are now in the third year of the war [against China], and the decisive time is coming at last. We Japanese must brace ourselves up and work much harder. . . . Please inform as many people as possible about "the benefits of reading a good magazine." In doing so, you could share the "bullets of the heart" with people and contribute to enhancing the power of our country.[4]

2. The other three earlier translations were Sanjin Kawa et al., "Kojiki Oji" (1898); Miekichi Suzuki, "Kojiki no Oji," (1925); and Hanako Muraoka, *Oji to Kojiki* (1934).

3. Shinsaku Hirata, "Nihon Moshi Tatakawaba!" (What if Japan fights the war); Shinsaku Hirata, "Showa Yugeki-tai" (Showa mobile forces); Jyuza Un'no, "Taiheiyo Raigeki Sentai" (The Pacific torpedo corps); Teiichi Muto, "Kotoshi wa Jugo Zentai no Senso da" (We will have total war with the home front this year).

4. Teiichi Muto, "Tsuyoku Tadashiki Kuni ni Sakae Are" (May the strong and just country prosper); Saburo Kawai, "Nihon e no Hakushu" (Applause to Japan);

In this atmosphere, a translation of an American novel situated in sixteenth-century England would obviously not be welcomed. However, *The Prince and the Pauper* was too attractive to be ignored even in this negative cultural climate. As a result, Osaragi, an expert in samurai stories, decided to "Japanize" the story. In the process, he transformed the democratic and antifeudalistic elements of Twain's original into forms more acceptable to Japanese readers, reflecting feudalistic and didactic cultural sentiments and the hierarchical social structure of prewar and wartime Japan.

Jiro Osaragi, born in Yokohama in 1897, was one of the most popular novelists in Japan from the 1920s to the 1940s. He was best known for his tremendously successful samurai novels, the *Kurama Tengu* series. The popularity of Kurama Tengu, the hero of the series, was perhaps equivalent to the popularity of Tarzan in America, which reached its zenith in the 1930s with the success of the film adaptations starring Johnny Weissmuller. However, Osaragi's literary output was not limited to his samurai novels. He also wrote serious novels situated in Europe and modern Japan, such as *Muteki* (Foghorn; 1934), *Nadare* (Avalanche; 1937), *Shijin* (Poet; 1946), *Kikyo* (Homecoming; 1949), and *Pari Moyu* (Paris Burning; 1964). In the postwar era, he was respected as a leading intellectual for his wide knowledge of Japanese and world history. His literary achievement was remembered after his death in 1973 with the establishment of the Osaragi Jiro Award to recognize the best Japanese nonfiction writing.

Osaragi shared Twain's sympathy toward victims of oppression. One of his stories was based on the case of Alfred Dreyfus, the Jewish lieutenant in France who was suspected of being a spy and sentenced to imprisonment for life. In this novel, *Dreyfus Jiken* (Dreyfus incident; 1930), Osaragi depicted the French militarists as blinded by their prejudice against Jews. As he stated later, this was his implicit criticism against the tyrannical Japanese militarists of the time.[5] In addition,

"Zasshi Shukan ni tsuite Onegai" (Requests concerning Magazine Week), *Shonen Kurabu* 26:10 (1939): 65.

5. Osaragi could read and write French and was familiar with French culture and history. His antimilitarist attitude was influenced by French literature, especially the works of Romain Rolland. His translations of essays and novels by Rol-

just as Twain increased his opposition to war and imperialism by criticizing the American colonization of the Philippines, the Japanese colonization of Asia raised Osaragi's indignation at the irrationality of militarism and colonialism. Although Osaragi could not publish his views in the prewar and wartime years because of government censorship, he privately wrote this about a trip to Southeast Asia, which had been colonized by Japan:

> There is no progress nor life in the world where people self-righteously believe that people will act only by order and the work has been finished by giving an order. Why has Japanese culture become so distorted, dried up, and powerless, and why was it forced on Asian people who wish to hold our hands as friends of Asia? As a result, Japan has become the object of hatred and indignation. We intentionally destroyed and corrupted Japanese culture which was originally beautiful, then after that, we forced it on them. No wonder they got angry.[6]

Osaragi therefore shared with Twain both a strong distaste for social injustice and sympathy toward the oppressed. It is no wonder that he was attracted to *The Prince and the Pauper,* in which these views are clearly expressed. Unfortunately, Japanese traditionalism was too strong for even a liberal writer like Osaragi to totally reject the conservative cultural climate and social system of imperial Japan.

Although Osaragi made no mention of it, "Hanamaru Kotorimaru" is obviously an adaptation of *The Prince and the Pauper.* Most of the main events in Twain's story appear in Osaragi's. Hanamaru is the young son of a samurai udaishō (captain general) who guards the Imperial Palace in Kyoto in the medieval era. Kotorimaru is the son of a pauper. Just as Edward VI and Tom Canty do in *The Prince and the Pauper,* Hanamaru and Kotorimaru note their remarkable resemblance to each other when they exchange clothes. When Hanamaru later tries to prove that he is really the heir of a noble samurai family, nobody believes him and he is taken for a lunatic. Some even think that he is haunted by a fox, since in Japanese superstition the fox in

---

land include *Clerambault* (1922), *Les Precurseurs* (1923), and *Pierre et Luce* (1924). See Koichi Fukushima, *Osaragi Jiro,* 1:105.

6. Ibid., 2:108–9.

human disguise is believed to deceive people. Misidentified as a pauper, Hanamaru experiences a life of poverty and danger. Just as Edward is almost killed by a mad hermit who believes himself to be an archangel, Hanamaru is almost killed by a mad priest who believes himself to be Fudomyo-o, the Buddhist god of fire. However, Hanamaru is not alone. Just as Edward has his guardian, Miles Hendon, Hanamaru has his royal vassal, Hachiro Otomo, a masterless samurai. Hachiro protects Hanamaru from his enemies, such as Kotorimaru's violent and drunken father, who tries to force Hanamaru to work as a beggar and a thief. Meanwhile, at the general's mansion, Kotorimaru is misidentified as the son of the general. The people at the mansion believe their master's son is mentally ill since he identifies himself as a pauper and acts like an uncivilized boy of the underclass, eating with his fingers and using vulgar language. In the end, too scared to participate in the funeral of the general, Kotorimaru escapes from the mansion and returns to his old familiar haunts. Hanamaru finds him, recovers his noble attire, and returns home. Although it is set in medieval Japan and its ending is slightly different, the main characters and plot of "Hanamaru Kotorimaru" are almost the same as those of *The Prince and the Pauper.* But the similarities between the two stories are not limited to characters and plot.

Among Twain's major works, *The Prince and the Pauper* is perhaps the most suitable for Japanese adaptation. To my knowledge, none of Twain's other major works have been adapted as book-length Japanese novels. There is no adaptation of *Tom Sawyer* or *Huckleberry Finn* that employs Japanese characters and settings. As discussed in the previous chapter, the absence of a Japanized Tom or Huck seems reasonable considering the difficulty of finding Japanese equivalents of the literary genre of bad-boy stories, American frontier villages, vast natural settings, and black slavery. But Japanese readers could easily understand the feudalistic society of sixteenth-century England. One significant reason that Osaragi could transform *The Prince and the Pauper* into a samurai story without much inconsistency is that both are set in a medieval, feudalistic society with a strict class hierarchy. In both stories the heroes behave differently according to their original social class, and the other characters' classist views are the source of the hardships the heroes face. Both stories also share the spirit and ethics of medieval monarchy. Just as Miles Hendon's loyalty to Edward is a reflection of chivalry in medieval Europe, Hachiro Otomo's loyalty to Hanamaru is based on Bushido, an ethic of chivalry founded upon samurais' spirit of loyalty to their sovereigns.[7] Because of these similarities, *The Prince and the Pauper* could be almost flawlessly transformed into a Japanese medieval samurai story.

However, the stories are also different in many ways. First, thanks to Twain's intensive research on the history of sixteenth-century England, *The Prince and the Pauper* is more detailed in its descriptions than is "Hanamaru Kotorimaru."[8] Twain incorporated a variety of historical characters and events in his narrative and succeeded in blending his imaginative fiction with the reality of history. His frequent references to such facts as the severe punishment doled out for trifling larcenies are particularly effective in lending historical reality to his satire of the cruelty of feudalism. Twain even added endnotes in order to provide readers with historical background. In contrast, "Hanamaru Kotorimaru" has virtually no historical characters and contains no references to historical facts. It is even impossible to specify in which century the story is situated. However, this does not mean that Osaragi neglected the historical reality in composing his story. On the contrary, Osaragi's consideration for historical reality might be one of the reasons for the absence of historical details in "Hanamaru Kotorimaru." A comparison of the two stories will help explain this paradox.

One of the significant differences between *The Prince and the Pauper* and "Hanamaru Kotorimaru" is in the status of its well-born heroes. While Edward is the son of the king, Hanamaru is the son of an udaishō, which, though a high samurai title in medieval Japan, is not as high as that of king of England. Udaishō in Japan did not have the political power that the king of England did. The Japanese emperor and shogun, the highest-ranking samurai, would be closer equivalents to the English king in terms of political and social status.

7. See Inazo Nitobe, *Bushido, the Soul of Japan: An Exposition of Japanese Thought.*

8. Twain's descriptions were also influenced by his extensive reading of French history. Everett Emerson writes, "[I]t was from [Hippolyte Taine's *The Ancien Regime*] that Mark Twain took the idea that the historian should assist the reader's imagination by providing detailed descriptions of architecture, costumes, the utensils of the hermit's hut, the grounds of the nobleman's estate." Everett Emerson, afterword to *The Prince and the Pauper,* 4.

It is clear why Osaragi could not make Hanamaru the son of an emperor. He published his story in a right-wing juvenile magazine in an era when fanatic worship of the royal family was evident throughout Japanese society, including schools and the mass media.[9] Many Japanese, particularly children, believed in the divinity of the emperor. In this atmosphere, Osaragi could not portray the son of an emperor living as a pauper among vulgar commoners. But why did he not portray Hanamaru as the son of the shogun, the second highest-ranking man in feudal Japan? As Americans had liberated themselves from the British king more than a hundred years before Twain wrote *The Prince and the Pauper,* the Japanese had liberated themselves from shogunate rule more than seventy years before Osaragi wrote his adaptation.[10] Therefore, he was under no obligation to refrain from portraying Hanamaru as the son of the shogun. However, there seems to have been at least one reason for him to avoid doing so.

The nationality of an author greatly influences his sense of distance from the history he deals with. As we have seen, Twain was very familiar with sixteenth-century English history. At the same time, however, we can assume that Twain enjoyed more distance from that history than could a native English author and felt no restrictions on the imaginative use of historical facts in his story. For an English author, perhaps, Henry VIII and Edward VI would seem too close and realistic to employ in such an unrealistic story as *The Prince and the Pauper.* Sure enough, the English reviews of the book were more critical than the American reviews. Many English reviewers expressed their dissatisfaction with Twain's unrealistic treatment of sixteenth-century England.[11] Unlike Twain, Osaragi was dealing with the history of his native country. As an author who was knowledgeable about Japanese history, he must have found it difficult to employ actual historical figures in his adaptation, and those with the highest titles, such as shogun or emperor,

9. In the January issue of *Shonen Kurabu* in which the first episode of "Hanamaru Kotorimaru" appeared, the editors listed ten virtues for their juvenile readers to follow. The first one was: "Respect our royal family, and love our country." "Shonen Kurabu Aidokusha no Sensei" (Declaration by *Shonen Kurabu* readers), *Shonen Kurabu* 26:1 (1939): 49.

10. Japan's feudalistic regime under the rule of shogun came to an end with the Meiji Restoration of 1868–1869.

11. See Emerson, afterword, 13.

would have seemed far too real to use in a highly imaginative novel. As a result, Osaragi decided to avoid all references to both actual historical events and characters, and he transformed Twain's historical story into an ahistorical romance. Edward VI, son of Henry VIII, became Hanamaru, son of the udaishō Kiyoharano Tokito, a completely fictional character. Perhaps if Osaragi had set his story in medieval China, for instance, he could have enjoyed enough distance from the historical reality to employ an emperor as a character, and his adaptation would have been much closer to Twain's original.

Osaragi neglected not only Twain's historical detail, but also his condemnation of feudalistic society. *The Prince and the Pauper* is a story of the cruelty and inhumanity of that society. In various scenes, Twain portrays injustice through Edward's eyes. Seeing a beggar being sold as a slave, the prince exclaims, "[T]his day the end of that law [of slavery] is come!" (*PP,* 214). Perhaps the cruelest scene in the novel is the execution of a Baptist woman who is burnt at the stake for her religious beliefs. Shocked by the sight, Edward sadly says, "That which I have seen, in that one little moment, will never go out from my memory, but will abide there; and I shall see it all the days, and dream of it all the nights, till I die. Would God I had been blind!" (*PP,* 327). Most of these descriptions were not adapted into "Hanamaru Kotorimaru." Moreover, although both Tom Canty as a mock king and Edward VI as a real king use their power to liberate the oppressed people, this aspect of reformation is also missing in Osaragi's adaptation.

One of the reasons for the absence of descriptions of cruelty in "Hanamaru Kotorimaru" must be Osaragi's consideration of the moral effect on juvenile readers, who were the main audience for his story. But another reason for this alteration was surely the oppressive social and cultural climate of wartime Japan. Wartime Japan, ruled by a tyrannical militaristic government, shared a certain cruelty with feudal England. The descriptions of imprisonment and execution for unjustifiable cause in *The Prince and the Pauper* overlap the historical accounts of oppression by the wartime Japanese government. During this era, a number of socialist and communist writers were imprisoned because of their antigovernment ideology. One of the worst cases was that of the proletarian writer Takiji Kobayashi, who was tortured to death in prison in 1933; other writers, editors, and intellectuals were also murdered by government officials for their thoughts and beliefs.[12] The imperial government imposed rigid censorship over publication and suppressed opinions critical of government policies. There is no proof that Osaragi intentionally avoided transposing Twain's critical descriptions of an oppressive political state into a Japanese setting so as not to offend an equally oppressive contemporary Japanese government. However, there was a tendency among writers in wartime Japan, particularly those who refused to endorse Japanese militarism and nationalism, to avoid making straightforward social criticisms and to confine their writings to a private world unrelated to larger issues of society and politics. Osaragi was one of these conscientious writers, and his adaptation of *The Prince and the Pauper,* a story of strong social criticism, reflects this tendency.

In a way, Osaragi transformed Twain's satire of feudalistic society into a story of personal moral development. The different perceptions that Edward and Hanamaru have of their hard experience as paupers demonstrates this transformation. Edward's experience as a pauper inspires him to seek the reform of feudalistic England. For instance, after being ridiculed by the rude boys at Christ's Hospital, he says to himself: "When I am king, they shall not have bread and shelter only, but also teachings out of books; for a full belly is little worth where the mind is starved, and the heart. I will keep this diligently in my remembrance, that this day's lesson be not lost upon me, and my people suffer thereby" (*PP,* 52–53). True to his pledge, Edward does not forget his lesson in the end. When he regains his title, he works to reform Christ's Hospital, unjust laws, and the cruel punishments he learned about in his journey as a pauper (*PP,* 399–401). Hanamaru, on the other hand, utilizes his hard experience as a pauper not for the reformation of society but for the development of his private ethics. When Hanamaru eats leftover cold rice and enjoys it, he feels ashamed of having been so picky about food in the palace and thinks, "[I]t must be just a matter of my eating habits that I am so spoiled when it comes to food" (HK, no. 10, 127–28). Then he perceives the episode as a lesson to

12. See Shigeo Hatanaka, *Nihon Fascism no Genron Dan'atsu Shoshi: Yokohama Jiken, Fuyu no Jidai no Shuppan Dan'atsu* (A brief history of the suppression of freedom of speech in Japanese fascism).

widen his narrow views. He says to Hachiro with deep feeling: "I have learned that there are a variety of people in this world. . . . I was not able to learn about those people before, because whenever I went out I was protected by vassals. Although this time, I have had a lot of hard experiences, I have learned a variety of things" (HK, 10:128).

Of course, these different perceptions are partly the result of differences in social status. Edward, as a future king, has enough political power to conduct a reformation of all of English society if he wants to. But Hanamaru is not the son of an emperor or shogun; he is just the heir of a noble samurai family. There is no way for him amass political power as great as Edward's and use it to reform society. Because of this limitation, Hanamaru is more concerned with the development of his own system of ethics than with the reformation of society. However, class difference is not the only reason for Osaragi's emphasis on the development of Hanamaru's ethics. Undoubtedly, private ethics is the most important theme of Osaragi's adaptation.

Morality and ethics are significant elements in both *The Prince and the Pauper* and "Hanamaru Kotorimaru." Both Twain and Osaragi carefully considered the moral effect of their stories on juvenile readers. As shown by its subtitle, "A Tale for Young People of All Ages," Twain did not intend *The Prince and the Pauper* only for children. However, it is also true that he considered young readers as its primary audience and valued their opinion of the story. Twain showed the manuscript not only to other writers, such as William Dean Howells, but also to the children of his friends. In addition, he originally planned to publish it in *St. Nicholas,* a leading juvenile magazine.[13] Twain's careful attention to his genteel juvenile readers was expressed explicitly in his dedication: "To those good-mannered and agreeable children Susie and Clara Clemens this book is affectionately inscribed by their father." As a result of his consideration of the book's moral effect on children, *The Prince and the Pauper*—unlike *Tom Sawyer* and *Huckleberry Finn,* which were banned from children's book sections in some libraries—was one of the least controversial of Twain's books in terms of its morality. Osaragi must also have considered his story's moral effect on juvenile readers, since "Hanamaru Kotorimaru" was

13. Emerson, afterword, 6–7.

serialized in a didactic juvenile magazine. During the wartime era, when the social atmosphere became dominantly conservative, the didacticism of *Shonen Kurabu* intensified. Stories and essays about good boys appeared side by side with installments of "Hanamaru Kotorimaru."[14] In a series of roundtable discussions titled "Honor Students Classroom," elementary school teachers introduced stories about model students.[15] The editors emphasized the positive ethical effect of the stories in *Shonen Kurabu.* For instance, they introduced Eiji Yoshikawa's samurai novel, which was serialized at the same time as "Hanamaru Kotorimaru," with these words from the author to his young readers: "I wrote this story hoping it will become a staff to sustain you when you start your career in the future. I put all my energy into writing this novel, looking forward to seeing you become great persons with great achievements in your careers. So please do not cast this staff away on your way to the future. If you think I have not tried hard to write this story, you can hit me with this staff. I promise this now." The editors added, "All the authors of other stories are writing like Mr. Yoshikawa, with similar intention and enthusiasm. We cannot help appreciating their great efforts."[16] It seems likely that Osaragi emphasized morality and ethics in his adaptation in deference to the editorial policy of the magazine.

In "Hanamaru Kotorimaru," the high ethical standards of the guardian Hachiro are particularly emphasized. Miles Hendon, the model for Hachiro, is also ethical, but he has an eccentric personality and is sometimes even savage. We can see this trait when he finds out the prince has gone from the inn. He shouts at the innkeeper, who is innocent of any

14. All the winning works in an essay contest in *Shonen Kurabu* featured model boys, including an apprentice barber who volunteers to trim the hair of poor boys every Sunday and a boy who forswears wearing socks in winter because he sympathizes with his soldier father who is fighting in the cold region of China. "Kon'na Kanshin na Shonen ga Aru" (We have such an admirable boy), *Shonen Kurabu* 26:1 (1939): 172–76.

15. "Yutosei Kyoshitsu: Anoko no ano Benkyo buri wo Kataru" (Honor students classroom: Talk on a student's method of study), *Shonen Kurabu* 26:10 (1939): 202–5.

16. "'Shonentachi no Tsue to Shitai': Yoshikawa Sensei no Ikigomi wo Kike" ("I want my work to be a staff for boys": Listen to Master Yoshikawa's eager words), *Shonen Kurabu* 26:2 (1939): 329.

wrongdoing: "Explain, thou limb of Satan, or thy time is come! . . . And so thou'rt a fool!—a fool, and easily cozened—hang all thy breed! . . . Out of my sight, idiot! Thy prating drives me mad!" (*PP,* 154–57). Hendon also likes to sing a song that seems to have indecent lyrics: "There was a woman in our town, / In our town did dwell / She loved her husband dearilee, / But another man he loved she, . . ." (*PP,* 152–54). In contrast, Hachiro is gentle in his behavior, and his words are more like those of a noble master of high ethics. For instance, he says to himself: "It is not so bad to be mad in this world full of people with corrupted spirits even though they are physically healthy. What is most significant is to have a healthy mind, and [Hanamaru] has it" (HK, 5:152). Elsewhere, Hachiro says to Hanamaru: "What is significant is not appearance but mind. It's natural that clothing will get dirty if you are poor. But, if you try hard, the mind will not get tainted no matter how poor you are" (HK, 9:101–2).

Hachiro is conscious of his role as moral teacher of Hanamaru. If necessary, he is willing to have Hanamaru endure hardship for his ethical improvement. For example, when some officers suspect Hanamaru of picking pockets, Hachiro lets them arrest him in order to teach him that everyone is equal under the law (HK, 9:108–9). Unlike Miles Hendon, Hachiro even neglects his subordinate role as Hanamaru's vassal when there is no other way to teach him. He determinedly persuades Hanamaru not to break into his father's funeral, saying: "Now, no lord nor vassal! . . . I cannot help preventing you from acting irrationally because you are a good boy. I will help you out of this situation, so just calm down and think it over!" (HK, 11:147–48).

For his part, Hanamaru accepts Hachiro's superiority as his moral teacher. He says: "How foolish man is. If I have a dirty appearance, people will never believe that I am Hanamaru, the son of Udaishō. . . . On the contrary, although he is poorly dressed, how great a person is Hachiro Otomo, that masterless samurai. . . . He sees not one's appearance but one's mind" (HK, 12:304). At the end of the story, after he is finally recognized as an heir of an udaishō family, Hanamaru respectfully addresses Hachiro as "sensei," which means both teacher and master (HK, 12:311).[17]

17. Hanamaru's respect for Hachiro reflects *Shonen Kurabu*'s idealistic image of its readers. In the aforementioned "Declaration by *Shonen Kurabu* Readers," the

In a way, this teacher-student relationship is also evident in the relationship between Osaragi and his juvenile readers. The editors of *Shonen Kurabu* flattered Osaragi by emphasizing his role as a teacher and casting his juvenile readers as his students. In response to a reader's letter, for instance, the editors wrote: "Osaragi-sensei is working very hard to write this novel, hoping to teach you a variety of things, such as the brave heart of Hanamaru who overcomes his hardship without losing his pride as a son of a noble samurai family and the obedient heart of Kotorimaru who is patiently waiting for the return of Hanamaru." In their concluding comments after the final installment of "Hanamaru Kotorimaru," the editors stressed its positive moral effects and called on readers to show their appreciation for the author's efforts: "We think that the honest mind of Hanamaru, who never lost his pride as a son of a noble samurai, must have been a great gift for you. Let us send our deep appreciation to the author, Osaragi-sensei, and the artist, Saito-sensei, for their great efforts for one year."[18] By emphasizing the elements of personal moral development and high ethics in Twain's original, Osaragi fulfilled the editors' expectation that he would assume the role of moral teacher of his juvenile readers.

In so doing, however, Osaragi weakened Twain's prince by transforming him into a more obedient character. While Edward assumes the throne with the political power to reform an entire society, Hanamaru is merely the son of a samurai, with much less political power, and an obedient student of his guardian's moral lessons. Obviously, Hanamaru was a much safer figure than Edward in wartime Japan where the patriarchal social hierarchy was still pervasive.

While in *The Prince and the Pauper* the social hierarchy under royal rule remains unchanged in the end, it is at the same time a story that breaks through class hierarchy. Although Tom Canty is a pauper at the bottom of that hierarchy, he is mentally much closer to the higher classes. From the beginning, Tom is depicted as unsatisfied. He feels ashamed of his dirty clothing. He teaches himself how to read and

---

third virtue was: "Respect your teachers and follow the opinion of those higher in age."

18. Editors' response to letter from Tomoko Kawashima, "'Hanamaru Kotorimaru' wo Yonde" (My impression of "Hanamaru Kotorimaru"), *Shonen Kurabu* 26:7 (1939), 336–37; editors' concluding comments, *Shonen Kurabu* 26:12 (1939): 311.

write in order to at least mentally liberate himself from the underclass to which he belongs. He daydreams about life in the royal court that he has read about in books and even imitates courtly manners (*PP*, 30–34). Later, when he is mistaken for the prince, Tom is quick to learn about court life and to assimilate to his new role. More importantly, he plans to employ his utmost political power as king to reform the oppressive feudal society. Immediately after the death of King Henry VIII, Tom announces to the Earl of Hertford "in a strong, earnest voice, and with great animation,—'Then shall the king's law be law of mercy, from this day, and never more be law of blood! Up from thy knees and away! To the Tower and say the king decrees the duke of Norfolk shall not die!'" (*PP*, 129). Tom even starts to enjoy court life, no longer worried about mocking the role of king. His state of mind during the days leading up to the coronation is explained as follows:

> [The] bright side [of court life] went on brightening more and more every day: in a very little while it was become almost all sunshine and delightfulness. He lost his fears; his misgivings faded out and died; his embarrassments departed, and gave place to an easy and confident bearing. . . .
>
> He came to enjoy being conducted to bed in state at night, and dressed with intricate and solemn ceremony in the morning. It came to be a proud pleasure to march to dinner attended by a glittering procession of officers of state and gentlemen-at-arms. . . . He liked to hear the bugles sounding down the long corridors, and the distant voices responding, "Way for the King!" (*PP*, 347–48)

Kotorimaru does not share Tom Canty's enthusiasm. He seldom enjoys his new life as an upper-class samurai, and he is always afraid of being revealed as a pauper. Unlike Tom, who begins to enjoy his role as king, Kotorimaru escapes from the palace and returns to his old familiar life. He tells his old friends: "Oh, I'm so happy! I've just run away from a stifling place. It's better for a pauper to live as a pauper. I've been so happy that I haven't been able to stop jumping since I came back here" (HK, 12:308). Unlike Tom, Kotorimaru is never able to adjust to life in the higher classes.

Of course, part of the reason for this difference between Kotorimaru and Tom is that an heir to an udaishō family does not have the same status as a prince or a king. The former is not a ruler of the country and does not have the unlimited political power of a king. At the same time, it should be much easier for Kotorimaru to play his part than it is for Tom to play his, since the son of a udaishō does not bear as much responsibility as a prince or a king. Even so, Kotorimaru is satisfied to remain a pauper in the end. Tom, thanks to his merciful reign as mock king, is promoted to the noble status of "King's Ward" (*PP,* 395). Unlike Kotorimaru, he succeeds in breaking through the rigid class hierarchy by dint of his own effort and ability.

Osaragi's treatment and characterization of his two heroes is hierarchical in comparison with Twain's more egalitarian treatment and characterization of Prince Edward and Tom Canty. Osaragi does not devote as much space to Kotorimaru as he does to Hanamaru. For instance, many episodes concerning the court life of Tom, such as the detailed description of his training in chapters 6 and 7 of *The Prince and the Pauper,* do not appear in Osaragi's adaptation. More importantly, Hanamaru is superior to Kotorimaru not only in his social class but also in his character and ability. For example, when Hanamaru finally finds Kotorimaru, who has run away from the palace and is playing happily with his fellow paupers, Kotorimaru cries from fear of punishment. Hanamaru soothes him and thanks him for being kind to the king during his absence (HK, 12:309–10). Here, Hanamaru's superiority is obvious; he is the mature and generous "big brother" and Kotorimaru is the fearful child. At the end of *The Prince and the Pauper,* on the other hand, Tom and Edward are depicted as equally mature and generous. Unlike the helpless Kotorimaru, who must be rescued by Hanamaru, Tom saves Edward from the life of a pauper by bravely and honestly revealing his own low birth and calmly surrendering the throne (*PP,* 370).

Osaragi seems to have accepted the hierarchical notion that personality depends on social class—that a person of noble birth will have a superior personality and a highly developed sense of dignity and a commoner will have an inferior personality and a weak mind. The socially superior Hanamaru has the ability to learn from his experience and grows both mentally and physically; he mentions that he has a much stronger body because of his hardship (HK, 12:305). But the socially inferior Kotorimaru is not competent to learn from his hardship, and remains a powerless pauper. Thus, Osaragi rejected Twain's egalitarian, democratic characterization of the protagonists of *The Prince and the Pauper.*

The rigidities of class hierarchy at a variety of levels in "Hanamaru Kotorimaru" provide another example of the Japanization of *The Prince and the Pauper.* Although Japan dismantled its rigid feudalistic class hierarchy as a result of the Meiji restoration in the mid-nineteenth century, the aristocratic titles remained until the end of World War II. Kazoku-rei, a law issued in 1884, conferred on aristocrats the titles of duke, marquis, earl, viscount, and baron and granted them a variety of social and financial privileges. Moreover, as depicted in Toson Shimazaki's naturalist novel *Hakai* (The broken commandment; 1906), many Japanese were severely prejudiced against the underclass and its descendants, called "buraku-min."[19] These rigid class distinctions are reflected in Osaragi's emphasis on class rigidity in "Hanamaru Kotorimaru."

In spite of or because of the Japanization of Twain's original, "Hanamaru Kotorimaru" was popular with Japanese readers. The letters from readers that appeared in the correspondence section of *Shonen Kurabu* testify that the appeal of "Hanamaru Kotorimaru" was not limited to boys. In one letter, a girl said, "'Hanamaru Kotorimaru' is the story which I read first whenever I opened the new issue of *Shonen Kurabu.*" Another letter, this time from a boy, said: "My mother is always the first reader of the new issue of *Shonen Kurabu.* She is a fan of 'Hanamaru Kotorimaru' and 'Michishio' and it is hard to take it from my mother until she finishes reading both stories." "Hanamaru Kotorimaru" was even enjoyed by grandmothers. One boy wrote: "Both my grandmother and mother liked 'Hanamaru Kotorimaru' more than any other stories in *Shonen Kurabu.* In the evening of the day when we receive *Shonen Kurabu,* all of our family usually sit in a circle around me and listen to my reading of 'Hanamaru Kotorimaru.' My grandmother is always looking forward to the next issue of *Shonen Kurabu,* worried about the future of both Hanamaru and Kotori-

19. *Hakai,* considered the first Japanese naturalist novel, deals with the plight of a village elementary school teacher who decides to reveal his underclass origin as a buraku-min. As a result, he is ostracized and loses almost everything. The novel was partly an adaptation of Dostoyevsky's *Crime and Punishment.*

maru."[20] "Hanamaru Kotorimaru" was too popular to disappear after its final installment in the magazine in December 1939. Just two years later, it was not only published in book form but was also made into a film, in which form it surely attracted a much larger audience.[21]

The wide acceptance of "Hanamaru Kotorimaru" surely owed to a variety of elements, including Osaragi's popularity as a writer, *Shonen Kurabu*'s large readership, and the reputation of Twain's original. However, the transformation or Japanization of Twain's story must also have contributed to its popularity. In making his adaptation, Osaragi took into account a variety of contemporary Japanese social and cultural trends, such as the boom in period novels, the decreasing popularity of translations of English and American literature, the fanatic respect for the royal family, the strong wartime didacticism, the suppression of political criticism, and the rigid class hierarchy in imperial Japan. This seems to explain why Seijiro Kojima's more faithful translation of *The Prince and the Pauper,* which was serialized in the same magazine in 1930, also in twelve installments, was not as popular as "Hanamaru Kotorimaru" would later be.[22]

The reception of Osaragi's adaptation demonstrates that the Japanese accepted Twain's works selectively and transformed them for their own purposes. At the same time, it shows that Twain had deeply penetrated into Japanese literature. Even in this anti-American and supernationalistic period, the Japanese did not isolate themselves from Twain's works. Thanks to the efforts of the critics, scholars, translators, and teachers who had kept him before the public for more than forty

20. Kawashima, "My Impression of 'Hanamaru Kotorimaru'"; Shin[?] Umemura, "Ikka Sorotte Aidokusha" (The whole family as avid readers), *Shonen Kurabu* 26:8 (1939), 339; Sueo Kawanishi, "Ikka Sorotte Aidokusha" (The whole family as avid readers), *Shonen Kurabu* 26:11 (1939), 313.

21. The book was brought out by a prestigious publisher, Chuokoron; see Jiro Osaragi, *Hanamaru Kotorimaru* (1941). After the war, two more editions were published; see Jiro Osaragi, *Hanamaru Kotorimaru* (1952) and *Hanamaru Kotorimaru/Suishoyama no Shonen* (Hanamaru Kotorimaru/The boys in Suishoyama; 1970). For the film adaptation, see *Hanamaru Kotorimaru,* dir. Shinzo Yoshida, and the article in the film journal *Eiga Junpo* (Cinema report) 20 (July 1941): 26. The film was reviewed in *Eiga Junpo* 24 (August 1941): 44. Unfortunately, the film is not stored in any film archive and cannot be seen today.

22. *Shonen Kurabu* printed no letters from readers praising Kojima's translation, in contrast to the many letters it printed praising Osaragi's adaptation.

years, Twain's works had become too appealing for a prestigious writer such as Osaragi to ignore and too widely disseminated for the Japanese public to avoid encountering them, even during this difficult era. In short, "Hanamaru Kotorimaru" testifies that Twain stays alive in Japan no matter how difficult the times and environment.

Just two years after the serialization of "Hanamaru Kotorimaru," Twain's works faced the most difficult social, cultural, and political environment yet in Japan. On December 8, 1941, Japan attacked Pearl Harbor and Twain's works became enemy literature in Japan from that day. Twain was neglected throughout World War II; no new translation of his works appeared and even references to Twain were few. To place the invisibility of Twain in context, it is necessary to look at the wartime suppression of literature, particularly juvenile literature and translations.

During the war, Japanese literature was under the absolute control of the government. The suppression of antigovernment writers became more severe and systematic as the Pacific war approached. For instance, in the same year as the attack on Pearl Harbor, the government-controlled Nihon Shuppan Bunka Kyokai (Japan Publishing Culture Association) required all publishers to submit proposed books for its approval. The association decided how much paper to allot based on how cooperative with government policy the books would be.[23] Needless to say, the more cooperative a proposed book was, the more paper its publisher would get. As a result of this strict control over the distribution of paper, publishers avoided translations of English and American books. Many Japanese writers were willing to support the wartime government. In the year of the attack on Pearl Harbor, they established an influential literary organization called Bungaku Hokoku Kai (Society of Literary Patriotism), with the slogan: "Join the forces of all Japanese writers in order to establish the Japanese literature that realizes the tradition and idealism of Imperial Japan and encourages its Imperial Culture."[24] As the war went on and the pub-

23. Nihon Shuppan Kyodo Kabushikigaisha, ed., *Shuppan Nenkan: Showa 17–nen ban* (Publication almanac, 1942), 38.

24. Jun Ezaki, "Bungaku Hokokukai Kessei made: *Bungei Nenkan* ni Miru Bungei Tosei" (Until the establishment of the Society of Literary Patriotism: The suppression of literature as seen in the *Literary Almanac*), 103.

lishing industry was nearly destroyed as a result of strict censorship, shortage of paper, and intensifying air raids, there was almost no other way for most Japanese writers to make a living than to cooperate with government policy. Even liberal writers who had translated Twain's works, such as Kuni Sasaki and Seijiro Kojima, participated in a series of patriotic lectures called Bungei Jugo Undo (Literary Home Front Movement), encouraging fatigued Japanese by providing literary and intellectual entertainment. Amid this atmosphere of fanatic nationalism, translations of enemy works were strictly suppressed. One year after the attack on Pearl Harbor, the almanac of the Japan Publishing Culture Association clearly demonstrated a negative attitude toward translation:

> We should be very careful about the publication of translations of world classics . . . when they were translated without much consideration to the current wartime situation. In particular, we will not be able to achieve victory without uniting all the power of our arms, economics, intelligence, and home front support. Therefore, "this is a world classic" could not be a reason convincing enough to permit the publication of a translation. We should examine the content of it to determine the suitability of its publication.[25]

Reflecting this hostile climate, translation projects of liberal English and French writers such as Maupassant, Joyce, Lawrence, and Huxley were ordered to be abandoned.[26] Wartime publication records of literature in translation show that the literature of Japan's allies replaced that of its enemies. Although French literature ranked first and German literature second in the number of Japanese translations in the first half of 1941, these rankings were reversed in the second half the year.[27] The popularity of German literature in Japan kept growing during the war. Japan Publishing Culture Association's 1943 almanac reported: "It is natural that new translations of English and American Literature hardly appeared [in 1942]. . . . In the sphere of the publication of the literature of juvenile translation, both English and American works were eliminated, and mainly German and Italian works were published instead." The suppression of translations of English

25. *Shuppan Nenkan: Showa 17-nen ban,* 40.
26. *Shuppan Nenkan: Showa 18-nen ban,* 61.
27. *Shuppan Nenkan: Showa 17-nen ban,* 39.

and American literature was not limited to new publications. English and American literature was even removed from the shelves of libraries.[28] The situation was best summarized in the postwar *Publication Almanac*:

> As the war became more fierce and difficult, the government Information Division controlled with fanatic suppression the whole sphere of Japanese publication. . . . Literature in translation was immediately suppressed, . . . and almost all English and American literature was suffocated under the name of literature of enemies. . . . What was characteristic about this era was the domination by national literature. The literary division of the Society of Literary Patriotism led this movement, . . . and celebrated the war of invasion with utmost traditionalism and supernationalism.[29]

The wartime suppression of English and American literature was a truly unusual phenomenon in terms of the history of modern Japanese literature. A number of Western literary classics had been models for Japanese writers before the war. In addition to English and American literature, French, German, and Russian literature played significant roles in the establishment and development of modern Japanese literature. For instance, Futabatei Shimei, who established the colloquial style of modern Japanese literature, was also an acclaimed translator of Turgenev and his style was greatly influenced by Russian literature. Soseki Natsume, perhaps the best-known and most respected modern Japanese writer, was a leading scholar and professor of English literature, and his works were undoubtedly founded upon his deep understanding and wide knowledge of Western literature. American literature, especially the transcendentalists and romantic writers of the mid-nineteenth century such as Emerson, Thoreau, Poe, and Whitman, had a great impact on modern Japanese writers who challenged the conservative norm of contemporary literary circles.[30] The Japanese nationalist writers who disregarded Western literature did not recognize the flexibility of modern Japanese literature in as-

28. *Shuppan Nenkan: Showa 18-nen ban,* 62; Takeshi Matsumoto, *Ryakudatsu Shita Bunka: Senso to Tosho* (The culture plundered: War and books), 154.
29. *Nihon Shuppan Nenkan: Showa 19–21-nen ban,* 19.
30. See Kamei, *From Meriken to America,* 174.

similating various elements of Western classics. Although the nationalist writers claimed they were returning to the tradition of Japanese literature, they failed to realize that they were in fact neglecting the cosmopolitanism of that tradition.

The fanatic nationalism of wartime Japan also had a great impact on Japanese juvenile literature. The government controlled juvenile literature as strictly as it did literature for adults. Three years before the outbreak of war, the government had set an official standard for juvenile literature, saying it "should be the literature which contributes to establish Japanese [habits of] mind, such as piety, loyalty, industriousness, honesty, faithfulness, modesty, courage, and affection." Works of juvenile literature that failed to meet this standard had little chance of being published during the war. It is no wonder that Twain's works, which frequently ridiculed this kind of didacticism and revealed its repressive effects on children, were avoided. In 1941, with the start of the war, the government-controlled Nihon Shokokumin Bunka Kyokai (Japan National Children's Culture Association) was established and top-down censorship of juvenile literature was intensified. Hideo Seki, a postwar advocate of democratic juvenile literature, later remembered the government's suppression of juvenile literature during the war. In a 1980 roundtable discussion, he said: "It is almost impossible to introduce in a short time all the examples of the Information Division's controls and oppressions on children's culture during the Pacific War. . . . At that time, we couldn't publish a book without putting a title [on it] such as 'Victory in the Pacific War!' . . . Otherwise, Japan Publishing Culture Association suppressed the manuscript and publication was indeed impossible."[31]

In this oppressive atmosphere, Twain almost disappeared from Japanese public spheres during World War II. Although there is no record of his works specifically being targeted, his books were naturally avoided as a result of nationalistic sentiment against Western classics

31. Michio Namekawa, *Nihon Jido Bungaku no Kiseki* (The locus of Japanese juvenile literature), 94; Hideo Seki, Mitsuo Ishikawa, and Tadamichi Kan, "Zadankai: Jido Bungaku wo Meguru Genron Yokuatsu no Rekishi" (Roundtable discussion: The history of the suppression of free speech in juvenile literature), 80.

(except those from Germany and Italy). In recognition of this sentiment, Kodansha, the country's largest publishing company, suspended its popular translation project of children's classics, *Kodansha Sekai Meisaku Zenshu* (Kodansha World Classic Series), in 1942.[32] Translations of *Tom Sawyer* and *The Prince and the Pauper,* which had been slated for the series, were put on hold, and a chance to maintain a large juvenile audience for these works was lost.

However, Twain was not entirely neglected during these years. The valuable exception was *Huckleberry Finn no Boken,* Tameji Nakamura's complete and faithful translation of *Adventures of Huckleberry Finn,* which appeared in 1941. Although Nakamura did not translate Huck's vernacular voice into equally vernacular Japanese, the book was finally accurately re-created in Japan fifty-six years after its publication in America.[33] Since Nakamura's translation was published in an inexpensive two-volume paperback edition by a prestigious publisher, Iwanami Shoten, it likely attracted a number of readers despite negative sentiment toward American literature. One Japanese boy who lived in a remote mountain village on Shikoku Island was greatly impressed with this edition of *Huckleberry Finn.* He read it at the age of nine during World War II. This boy's name was Kenzaburo Oe; he would later become an acclaimed writer and Nobel Prize laureate in literature. In a 1999 interview, Oe remembered his first encounter with *Huckleberry Finn:*

> I didn't read many books before nine years old. I was fascinated by the telling of tales of my grandmother. She was talking about almost everything about my family and my district; so it was enough for me. I didn't need any books at that time. But one day, there was some discussion between my grandmother and my mother. And my mother got up very early in the morning, and she packed one kilogram of rice . . . and she went to the small city of our island through the forest. Very late at night she returned. She gave a small doll to my sister, and some cakes for my younger brother, and she took out two pocket books. Tome one, tome

32. Kodansha, *Kodansha 70nen-shi, Sengo-hen* (Seventy years of Kodansha, Post–World War II period), 88.

33. For more on Nakamura's translation, see Yoshio Katsuura, *Hon'yaku no Konjaku: Mark Twain no Kotoba, Nihon-jin no Kotoba* (Translations then and now: Mark Twain's language and Japanese people's language), 255–66.

> two. I found Mark Twain's *Huckleberry Finn.* I didn't know the name of Mark Twain, the name of Tom Sawyer or Huckleberry Finn, but my mother said—and this was the first talk between my mother and I about literature, and almost the last talk. She said, "This is the best novel for a child or for an adult. Thus your father said." (The year before my father had passed away.)[34]

Oe next remembered how Twain's works were suppressed during the war. His mother said to him: "I brought this book for you, but the woman who made the barter with the rice between us said, 'Be careful. The author is American. Now the war between U.S. and Japan is going on. The teacher will take the book from your son. [Tell him] that if your teacher asks you who is the author, you must answer that Mark Twain is the pseudonym of a German writer.'" After the war, Oe read *Huckleberry Finn* again, this time in English, and called it a work that "opened the door to the world of literature."[35] In her book on Twain, Shelley Fisher Fishkin quotes Oe's translator John Nathan as saying: "It was Huck's moral courage, literally Hell-bent, that ignited his imagination. For Oe the single most important moment in the book was always Huck's agonized decision not to send Miss Watson a note informing her of Jim's whereabouts and to go instead to Hell. With that fearsome resolution to turn his back on his times, his society, and even his god, Huckleberry Finn became the model for Oe's existential hero." Oe has happily admitted that his works were greatly influenced by his reading of *Huckleberry Finn.* When Fishkin met Oe in Austin, Texas, he wrote in her copy of *Nip the Buds, Shoot the Kids*: "Yes, I agree with your opinion about Huck, the narrative of my first novel is under the shadow of Huck."[36] Shoji Goto has suggested that since Oe's works

34. Harry Kreisler, "Art and Healing," interview with Kenzaburo Oe, April 16, 1999, Institute of International Studies, University of California at Berkeley, http://globetrotter.berkeley.edu/people/Oe/oe-con1.html.

35. Ibid.; Oe, "Toni Morrison and *Adventures of Huckleberry Finn.*"

36. Nathan quoted in Fishkin, *Lighting Out for the Territory,* 190; Shelley Fisher Fishkin, e-mail to author, October 27, 2002. Although their endings are quite different, there are many similarities between *Huckleberry Finn* and "Shiiku" (The catch), Oe's early short story, such as the employment of a village boy as a narrator, the imprisonment of a genial black man, the development of a friendship between an innocent boy and a black man, and the portrayal of severe racism against blacks.

have had a tremendous impact on postmodern Japanese literature, *Huckleberry Finn* had a hand in the development of Japanese literature through Oe.[37] Thus, Oe's fascination with *Huckleberry Finn* proves that Twain's works have never ceased to provide creative energy to the Japanese people, even during the difficult era of wartime anti-Americanism.

37. Shoji Goto, "Huck Finn and America in Kenzaburo Oe," 40.

3

Mark Twain in Postwar Japan

Juvenile Translations and School Textbooks

Tom Sawyer and *Huckleberry Finn* were two of the most frequently published American novels in postwar occupied Japan. Why were these novels so popular during the occupation? Did the Japanese accept them as they were, or did their translators transform them to reflect the cultural climate of Japanese society under the pressures of American democratization? The answers to these questions can be found by focusing on a variety of Japanese juvenile translations of *Tom Sawyer* and *Huckleberry Finn.*

After the end of the war, Japan ended its long suppression of American culture and literature and started the tremendous push toward Americanization of its society and culture. During this era, America had a great impact on every sphere of Japanese life. The American-dominated General Headquarters (GHQ) held the political power in occupied Japan and led the "democratization program." It started by eliminating the source of militaristic nationalism and anti-Americanism in Japan. The emperor renounced his divinity and nearly a thousand war criminals, including military leaders, were executed by decision of the Tokyo Trial led by the Allied powers. GHQ censored virtually all Japanese publications, films, and radio programs, suppressing elements of militarism, nationalism, and anti-Americanism.[1]

GHQ also carefully selected the American cultural products to be disseminated in Japan. Films that depicted the underside of American society, such as *The Grapes of Wrath,* were avoided.[2] Translations were under the control of the Supreme Command for the Allied Powers (SCAP) Translation Program, which selected suitable books to be translated into Japanese for the first time. GHQ recommended *Animal Farm* for its "satire on dictatorship," which, it was thought, would contribute to the democratization of Japan.[3] Through this program, 3,550 books were translated into Japanese during the occupation, the majority of which were American books.[4]

As far as Twain's influence on Japan during the occupation era is concerned, his impact was still largely limited to the sphere of Japanese children's literature. As in other cultural spheres, America greatly influenced the democratization of Japanese children's literature, and a number of postwar writers, editors, and critics of that literature either spontaneously or reluctantly cooperated with GHQ's democratization policy. Immediately after the war, for instance, a variety of so-called democratic children's magazines appeared, and Nihon Jido Bungakusha Kyokai (the Japanese Writers of Children's Literature Association) was founded under the slogan "Create and spread democratic

1. John Dower, *Embracing Defeat: Japan in the Wake of World War II,* 80–84, 447.

2. Tanigawa, *American Films and Occupation Policy,* 444–45.

3. GHQ's Civil Information and Education Division (CI&E) reported the book's publication as follows: "*Animal Farm,* George Orwell's very readable satire on the methods of a dictatorship, has come out in Japanese under SCAP Translation program. For reading by both old and young who are befogged by the utopian claims of authoritarian ideology, it can be recommended with enthusiasm." "*Animal Farm* Is Published in Japanese," *CI&E Semimonthly Bulletin,* June 22, 1949, 7, National Diet Library, Tokyo.

4. Of the 1,087 copyrighted books translated through the SCAP Translation Program, 733 (or 67 percent) were American, 117 French, 101 British, 49 German, and 87 from other countries. "Totals Are Given for Foreign Books Published in Japan under SCAP Translation Program," *CI&E Semimonthly Bulletin,* October 12, 1949, 5.

children's literature."[5] Hideo Seki, the leader of the association, announced its founding by emphasizing the new climate: "The only way for the children's writers to become guardians of the free minds of children is to understand this democratic revolution and become aware of their responsibilities to accomplish it."[6]

The democratization of Japanese children's literature was not entirely spontaneous, however; it was under the control of the American-dominated GHQ. Although it tried not to be heavy-handed, GHQ censored anti-American, militaristic, and nationalistic elements in children's literature. It also employed juvenile literature as a means to spread positive images of America. GHQ's Civil Information and Education Section (CI&E) started the Gift Book Program to introduce "Democratic America" to Japanese children and teachers.[7] In this program, members of the U.S. Education Mission and American librarians selected more than seven hundred books that they believed would contribute to the elimination of prejudice against America by introducing the Japanese to the American way of life. The books were exhibited in major cities, drawing 250,000 Japanese in Tokyo alone in February 1947.[8] After the exhibitions, they were distributed as gifts, mainly to school libraries. Mitsuo Ishikawa, the editor of one of the leading juvenile magazines during the occupation, later described how he was pressured to help publicize these books:

> At that time, more than a few times a month, CI&E asked me to publish the works of American children's literature that the American government purchased. They said, "We will give those works out free, so why don't you publish them in your magazine." Of course, they were the works that introduced only the favorable side of America. I sometimes translated and published these works because it was unacceptable to

5. Hideo Seki, "Minshushugi Jido Bungaku no 30-nen" (Thirty years of Japanese juvenile literature), 15. For a description of the new "democratic" juvenile magazines, see Kan, *Japanese Juvenile Literature,* 349–53.

6. Hideo Seki, "Jido Bungaku sha wa Nani wo Nasubeki ka" (What should writers of juvenile literature do?), 7.

7. *Asahi Shimbun* (Asahi newspaper), April 3, 1946, sec. 2.

8. Yuriko Nakamura and Taro Miura, "Senryoki ni okeru Kyouiku Shisetsudan karano 'Hon no Okurimono'" (The gift books from the U.S. Education Mission during the occupation era), 53, 55, 60.

> simply turn down their offers all the time. If I didn't publish them, they were in a very bad mood.[9]

In this atmosphere of American democratization, Mark Twain came back to Japan. An edition of *The Adventures of Tom Sawyer* illustrated by Norman Rockwell was one of the books sent to Japan by the Gift Book Program.[10] Twain was also one of the American writers whose works were most frequently translated into Japanese during the occupation. *Democracy in the Classroom,* a leading postwar Japanese educational journal, reported that ten translations of Twain's works appeared within three years after the end of the war, which was the largest number of translations among American writers. The second most translated American writer during that span was Louisa May Alcott, with eight translations. *Tom Sawyer* was one of the most frequently translated American works of the time. Five Japanese *Tom Sawyer*s appeared during the occupation, a total equaled only by *Uncle Tom's Cabin.*[11] Although it was unimaginable for the heavily didactic prewar Japanese school textbooks to employ Twain's works, *Tom Sawyer* was adopted as a part of many postwar Japanese textbooks. In addition, the Kodansha World Classic Series, the massive translation project that was suspended during the war, started up again during the occupation and *Tom Sawyer, The Prince and the Pauper,* and *Huckleberry Finn* were all eventually included in the series.[12] For grown-up readers, Eiji Ishida's faithful translation of *Tom Sawyer* was published immediately after the war as a paperback edition by Iwanami Shoten, one of the most prestigious Japanese publishers. Iwanami also republished its faithful translations of *Huckleberry Finn* and *The Prince and the Pauper* in paperback editions during the occupation era.[13]

9. Seki, Ishikawa, and Kan, "Roundtable Discussion," 87.

10. Madoko Kon, "Amerika Kyouiku Shisetsudan no Okurimono" (The tribute from the U.S. Education Mission), 127.

11. "Shiryo" (Materials), *Seikatsu Gakko* (English title: *Democracy in the Classroom*) 3:8 (1948): 47–59.

12. Kuni Sasaki, trans., *Tom Sawyer no Boken* (1950); Katsuhiko Otaguro, trans., *Kojiki Oji* (1950); Kuni Sasaki, trans., *Huckleberry no Boken* (1951). See also Kodansha, *Kodansha no 80 nen* (Eighty years of Kodansha), 254–55.

13. Eiji Ishida, trans., *Tom Sawyer no Boken* (1946); Tameji Nakamura, trans., *Huckleberry Finn no Boken* (1941, reprint, 1950); Hanako Muraoka, trans., *Oji to Kojiki* (1934; reprint, 1950).

This time, *Tom Sawyer* and *Huckleberry Finn* were welcomed more readily than *The Prince and the Pauper.* Translations of *Tom Sawyer* or *Huckleberry Finn* outnumbered those of *The Prince and the Pauper* for the first time in Japan. As of October 1948, five editions of *Tom Sawyer,* three of *Huckleberry Finn,* and two of *The Prince and the Pauper* were published.[14]

There seem to be several reasons for the popularity of *Tom Sawyer* and *Huckleberry Finn* during the occupation era. In America, the popularity of these books had already surpassed that of Twain's other works. The reputation of *Huckleberry Finn* in particular thrived in the United States in the 1930s and '40s thanks to some influential literary critics.[15] Japanese publishers, translators, and readers, who were finally allowed access to American magazines and journals, might have been influenced by the American reputations of both works.

It also seems probable that the Japanese, who lived with the idea of American democratization, would prefer *Tom Sawyer* and *Huckleberry Finn,* stories about democratic American boys, to *The Prince and the Pauper,* a story about medieval feudalistic England. Tsunatake Furuya, an influential critic of postwar Japanese juvenile literature, regarded *Tom Sawyer* and *Huckleberry Finn* as models for writers to follow. In his influential essay "Jido Bungaku e no Yobo" (Requests to juvenile literature), which appeared in the first issue of a new educational journal immediately after the war, Furuya stated that *Tom Sawyer* and *Huckleberry Finn* were two of the best works of children's literature because they transcended the boundary between artistic and popular literature. He called for a postwar Japanese juvenile literature that was both artistic and entertaining, like *Tom Sawyer* and *Huckleberry Finn.*

14. "Materials," 52–53; Yoshio Sekino, Yoshio Nakano, et al., "Hon'yaku Seishonen Tosho no Shomondai" (Problems in the books of juvenile translations), 5.

15. Bernard DeVoto in the 1930s and Lionel Trilling in the 1940s played significant roles in establishing the reputation of Twain's works in America. DeVoto, an editor of the influential *Saturday Review of Literature,* countered Van Wyck Brooks's underestimation of Twain by publishing *Mark Twain's America* (1932) and articles that extolled Twain's genius in creating literature from American frontier experiences and cultures. For a discussion of Twain's reputation, see Roger Asselineau, *The Literary Reputation of Mark Twain from 1910 to 1950: A Critical Essay and a Biblography.* For Trilling's role, see Arac, *Huckleberry Finn as Idol and Target,* 108–32; and Tsuyoshi Ishihara, "20-seiki America Zasshi ni okeru Mark Twain-zo: Shoshi-teki Kenkyu" (Images of Mark Twain in twentieth-century American popular magazines: A bibliographical study).

He particularly valued the spontaneous expression in both works of the abundant energy of life (*seimei-ryoku*), which, he said, was seldom found in Japanese juvenile literature. In this way, Furuya used *Huckleberry Finn* and *Tom Sawyer* as springboards for the emancipation of Japanese juvenile literature from its prewar and wartime didacticism and repression of spontaneity.[16]

During the occupation, Huck was regarded as an American democratic hero, and Japanese juvenile translators sometimes emphasized images of individual freedom in their work. One translator even added to the title *Adventures of Huckleberry Finn* a subtitle not found in the original: *An American Boy Who Sought Freedom.*[17] However, with democratization under the strict control of the American occupation army, it was necessary to transform both *Huckleberry Finn* and *Tom Sawyer* in other ways as well.

One of the main transformations was the deletion of the elements of violence in the originals. This practice reflected American occupation policy. GHQ's Civil Censorship Detachment (CCD) strictly censored portrayals of violence in Japanese publications, films, theatrical productions, and radio programs. For instance, an illustration that appeared in the juvenile magazine *Shokokumin no Tomo* (Friends for the children of the nation) a year after the end of the war earned the disapproval of GHQ censors. The accompanying article emphasizes the importance of thinking critically and individually rather than blindly following the orders of authorities. The illustration showed a marching robot connected to a control box operated by a soldier; the connection to a second soldier's control box has been broken. The caption

16. Tsunatake Furuya, "Requests to Juvenile Literature." Shin Torigoe has also referred to Japanese juvenile literature's failure to entertain: "[T]he recently deceased literary critic, Sei Ito, defined the characteristics of Japanese literature as 'literature of ethics.' Japanese juvenile literature is no exception. It has been a 'literature of ethics' all the more for its close relation with education. In short, there has been no literary tradition of entertainment in Japanese juvenile literature." Shin Torigoe, "Sengo Jido Bungaku no 50-nen wo Gaikan Suru: Futatabi Meguttekita Kiki no Jidai no Naka de" (Survey of the fifty years of juvenile literature after World War II: In the time of crisis which has returned), 16. See also Torigoe, "Immaturity of Adventure Novels," 251.

17. Naotaro Tatsunokuchi, trans., *Huckleberry Finn no Boken: Jiyu wo Motometa America Shonen* (1948).

in the box reads: "Never turn out a nation like a robot which moves at one's command" (fig. 3). Since the soldier who is manipulating the robot looks like an American GI and the one who has lost control resembles a Japanese soldier, the illustration could have been seen as a challenge toward the authority of the American occupation army. As a result, GHQ suppressed both illustration and caption, labeling them "'Divine Land' propaganda" (fig. 4).

Although American oversight of juvenile literature was not as strict as that of other literary genres, translators of *Tom Sawyer* and *Huckleberry Finn* clearly felt compelled to engage in self-censorship. In the censored Japanese publications held in the Gordon W. Prange Collection at the University of Maryland, one finds the notations of GHQ censors: "Suppress," "Delete," "Hold," "OK," and "Approved." In the juvenile translations of Twain's works, however, the only notations are "OK" and "Approved." Since these translations passed through GHQ with no problem, it is obviously the translators and not the censors who were responsible for any alterations and deletions. Shogo Koide's postwar translation of *Tom Sawyer* completely omits the sadistic Dobbins's corporal punishment of his students. In Kuni Sasaki's prewar translation, the scene remains intact; in prewar Japan, as in nineteenth-century America, corporal punishment was a common and accepted means to enforce discipline among students.[18] When it comes to descriptions of violence, though, *Huckleberry Finn* is more brutal than *Tom Sawyer. Huckleberry Finn* has scenes of murder, lynching, child abuse, and fighting stemming from a family feud. These descriptions were avoided in Japanese translations. Although *Huckleberry Finn* was also bowdlerized in prewar translations, the postwar translators went further. For example, in his postwar translation *Yadonashi Huck no Boken* (The adventures of homeless Huck; 1950), Koide omitted Twain's detailed descriptions of bloody fighting between the Shepherdsons and the Grangerfords, instead summarizing the feud in just a few lines (*YH*, 58). He also deleted even brief references to guns. The judge's remark about Pap—"he reckoned a body could reform the ole man with

18. Shogo Koide, trans., *Meisaku Monogatari: Tom Sawyer no Boken* (Classic story: *The Adventures of Tom Sawyer;* 1948); Kuni Sasaki, trans., "Tom Sawyer," in *Mark Twain Meisaku Shu* (Selected works of Mark Twain; 1929), 250–51.

Fig. 3. *Shokokumin no Tomo,* October 1946, 14. Gordon W. Prange Collection, University of Maryland, part 1, Microfilm of Censored Periodicals: 1945–1949, reel 224.

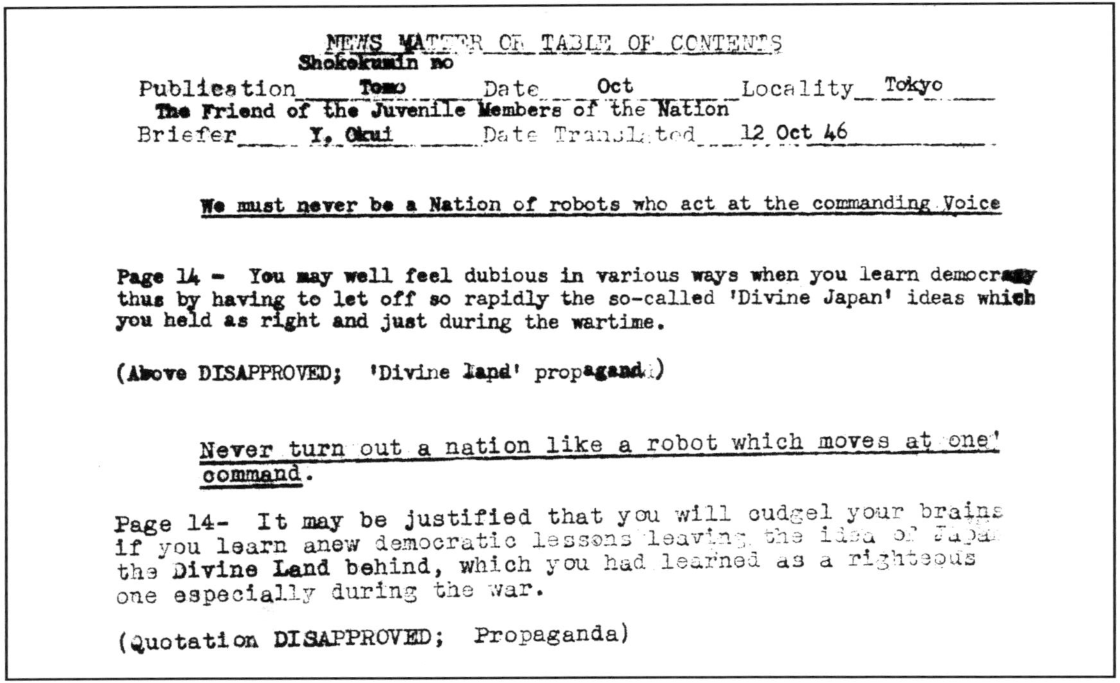

NEWS MATTER OR TABLE OF CONTENTS

Shokokumin no

Publication Tomo Date Oct Locality Tokyo

The Friend of the Juvenile Members of the Nation

Briefer Y. Okui Date Translated 12 Oct 46

We must never be a Nation of robots who act at the commanding Voice

Page 14 - You may well feel dubious in various ways when you learn democracy thus by having to let off so rapidly the so-called 'Divine Japan' ideas which you held as right and just during the wartime.

(Above DISAPPROVED; 'Divine Land' propaganda)

Never turn out a nation like a robot which moves at one' command.

Page 14- It may be justified that you will cudgel your brains if you learn anew democratic lessons leaving the idea of Japan the Divine Land behind, which you had learned as a righteous one especially during the war.

(Quotation DISAPPROVED; Propaganda)

Fig. 4. Censorship document dated October 12, 1946, showing that the illustration and caption in figure 3 were "disapproved." Gordon W. Prange Collection, University of Maryland, part 1, Microfilm of Censored Periodicals: 1945–1949, reel 224.

a *shot-gun,* maybe"—was deleted, as was the scene in which Huck points a gun at his violent father in order to protect himself (*YH,* 30, 35).

Japanese juvenile translations of other American classics also tended to omit descriptions of violence. *Uncle Tom's Cabin,* one of the most popular American books in Japan, was tamed considerably, with Harriet Beecher Stowe's descriptions of the brutality of slaveholders softened and shortened in most translations.[19] In a 1948 roundtable discussion, the translator Yoshio Nakano referred to the reason behind this bowdlerization when he said, "[W]e are facing a slightly delicate situation nowadays, and those Japanese translators [omitted descriptions of the cruel treatment of slaves] considering that situation."[20] The "delicate situation" was obviously the American censorship of elements of violence. Nakano was undoubtedly familiar with this situation, since he was one of fourteen officially selected supervisors of translations of books that GHQ approved for publication in Japanese.[21] Direct reference to American censorship was prohibited during the occupation, but Nakano's comment points to Japanese juvenile translators' tendency to self-censor elements of violence and feudalistic cruelty in consideration of the censors.

Even after the suppression of descriptions of violence in *Tom Sawyer* and *Huckleberry Finn,* however, the heroes of both stories were still considered dangerous by Japanese moral guardians. Both Tom and Huck could be seen as versions of the juvenile delinquents that plagued Japan after the war. Street children and juvenile delinquents were two of the most serious social problems in postwar Japan. Many children who lost their parents during the war preferred the freedom of the street to life in an orphanage or the home of a relative. In 1947 there were 5,635 street children in Japan.[22] Delinquent behaviors such as underage smoking and stealing were common among these children. In fact, they shared a number of characteristics with Huck Finn.

19. Yutaka Fukuda, "Mittsu no Uncle Tom Monogatari" (Three translations of *Uncle Tom's Cabin*), 24.

20. Sekino et al., "Problems in the Books of Juvenile Translations," 9.

21. *Nihon Shuppan Nenkan: Showa 22,23-nen ban* (Japan publication almanac, 1947–1948), 3.

22. Toshio Takeda, "Furoji no Tanjo" (The emergence of street children), 3.

As Fumiko Hayashi, a leading Japanese writer of the time, put it, they were "lazy," "hated cleaning," "seldom studied and worked," "liked to lie down and relax," and "told lies about who they were and where they came from."[23]

Japanese translators were apprehensive that Tom and Huck might help to justify juvenile delinquency among street children. In the afterword of his translation of *Tom Sawyer,* Shogo Koide explained the reasons for his bowdlerization of the original. He wrote: "Considering the present situation after the war when not only unfortunate street children but also ordinary children at home get into vicious habits, influenced by the moral confusion of our society, we should be very careful about provocative stories for juvenile readers in Japan."[24] Worried about bad influences on children, Koide omitted the scene in *Tom Sawyer* in which Huck teaches Tom and Ben Rogers how to smoke. In Koide's translation of *Huckleberry Finn,* naturally, the bowdlerization was more thorough. Following the tradition of Sasaki's prewar juvenile translations, Koide never shows Huck stealing or using vulgar language. Moreover, while even the genteel Huck of prewar Japanese translations liked to smoke,[25] Koide's Huck is totally free from this habit. Where Twain's Huck says, "It was kind of lazy and jolly, laying off comfortable all day, smoking and fishing, and no books nor study" (*HF,* 46), Koide's Huck says, "It was lazy and jolly, fishing all day and no books" (*YH,* 9). Twain's Huck says, "I laid there [in the canoe], and had a good rest and a smoke out of my pipe, looking away into the sky, not a cloud in it" (*HF,* 59), but Koide's Huck says, "I laid there, looking away into the sky, not a cloud in it" (*YH,* 38).

The postwar translations of *Tom Sawyer* and *Huckleberry Finn* also demonstrate the limitations of the American democratization of Japan. GHQ was encouraging Japanese filmmakers to include Hollywood-style love scenes in their films. Vivid images of equal relationships between men and women, it was hoped, would discourage the "undemocratic" and "feudalistic" repression of love in traditional Japanese society. Kissing scenes began to appear for the first time in Japanese films,

23. Fumiko Hayashi, "Furoji" (Street children). See also Dower, *Embracing Defeat,* 61–64.

24. Koide, afterword to *Meisaku Monogatari,* 186.

25. See Seika Shibusawa, trans., *Tom Sawyer no Boken* (1933), 108–12.

becoming secular symbols of democracy for the public.[26] However, this particular aspect of American democratization had no effect on the rigorous tradition of chasteness in Japanese juvenile translations. Just as in the genteel prewar translations, the scenes in which Tom and Becky say "I love you" and exchange kisses were entirely deleted in Koide's translation. Even Huck's more innocent expressions of admiration for Mary Jane Wilks were eliminated in postwar translations.

At the same time, postwar Japanese juvenile translators idealized Huck Finn rather than Tom Sawyer, reflecting the cultural climate of democratization. Huck's adventures on the raft generate images of unfettered freedom, and, more importantly, Huck works for the freedom and equality that are the foundation of democracy but that are denied in a feudalistic slaveholding society. In short, Huck had more democratic potential than did Tom Sawyer. Keisuke Tsutsui, in his translation *Huckleberry no Boken* (Adventures of Huckleberry; 1948), overestimated Huck's potential as an idealistic democratic hero. Tsutsui claimed in his introduction that he translated *Huckleberry Finn* "only for the children, who will contribute to the democratization of Japan in the future" (*HB,* 1). In the translation itself, he emphasized democratic images of freedom and equality. In a well-known scene in the original, Huck, having finally escaped from his tyrannical father, lies down in his canoe to smoke his pipe, ruminating on the deepness of the night sky and the snatches of conversation that are audible from the shore. In Tsutsui's translation, however, Huck says nothing about nighttime sights or sounds. Instead, he simply says with deep emotion, "How free I am" (*HB,* 29). Although it is impossible to decipher the exact intention behind this alteration, the emotion expressed by Tsutsui's Huck would have been shared by the postwar Japanese, who were finally emancipated from their militaristic rulers.[27]

26. Hirano, *Mr. Smith Goes to Tokyo,* 154–70.

27. Many intellectuals shared a sense of freedom from wartime oppression. Sozo Matsuura, an editor of the liberal magazine *Kaizo* (Reconstruction), said: "The happiest day of my life was August 15, 1945, the day we lost the Pacific War. . . . It is no exaggeration to say that Japan under the prewar Meiji constitution was a hell for anyone with the slightest desire to think freely." Quoted in Jay Rubin, "From Wholesomeness to Decadence: The Censorship of Literature under the

Tsutsui also made Twain's criticisms of cruelty and violence more explicit. His alteration of Huck's response to the bloody fight between the two feuding families, the Shepherdsons and the Grangerfords, demonstrates this. While Twain's Huck is silent after the fight, Tsutsui's Huck makes a clear pacifist statement, saying, "I thought that things like revenge are truly foolish, because even a good boy like [Buck] could be a victim of it" (*HB*, 112). Although Twain's Huck would agree with this statement, it weakens Twain's literary art, which conveyed the same message without direct statement. However, the explicit denouncement of vengeance in Tsutsui's translation was a better fit for the cultural climate of postwar Japan than the implied denouncement in Twain's original. GHQ was very sensitive about Japanese stories of vengeance. For example, *Chushingura, or the Forty-Seven Ronins,* a popular story about samurais taking revenge on behalf of their master, was prohibited for a while after the war since it was regarded as "undemocratic" and "feudalistic."[28] The episode of the bloody feud in *Huckleberry Finn* is as "undemocratic" as anything in *Chushingura.* The southern quasi-aristocratic families act collectively, ignoring people's rights before the law; they are quick to kill their enemies (even an adolescent boy) in order to protect the reputations of their families and satisfy their desire for revenge. No wonder that in Tsutsui's translation, published in an environment defined by the democratization movement's explicit assertions of American ideals, Huck clearly criticizes the families' undemocratic acts of cruel violence.

It is Tsutsui's treatment of the relationship between Huck and Jim that best shows his idealization of Huck as the perfect democratic hero. In Twain's original, Huck is familiar with the strict rules of slaveholding society, in which to assist a runaway slave is regarded as one of the greatest sins. As a result, he struggles between the pull of his friendship with Jim and that of his conscience as a white boy nurtured in the

---

Allied Occupation," 75. The literary critic Mitsuo Nakamura wrote at the end of the occupation era, "Among the various 'freedoms' that the American occupation provided to Japanese citizens, the 'freedom' provided to writers was substantial, and it was incomparable to the very strict prewar and wartime censorship." Mitsuo Nakamura, "Senryoka no Bungaku" (Literature under the occupation), 507–8.

28. Hirano, *Mr. Smith Goes to Tokyo,* 66–70.

slaveholding South. Twain's Huck is not a perfect democrat who can reject society's unfair rules without any hesitation. More than a few times, he decides to turn Jim in, obeying his "deformed conscience." Tsutsui's Huck, however, is completely unfettered by the undemocratic rules of a slaveholding society. On a psychological level, he is not a typical white southern boy of the time. Unlike Twain's Huck, he never doubts the justice of helping Jim out of slavery, and he is never stung by a "deformed conscience." In order to construct the image of a Huck who is free from racial prejudice, Tsutsui made Huck's feelings toward Jim more explicit. For instance, in the scene where Huck runs away from the feud and reunites with Jim, Tsutsui added sentimental remarks to the original, such as, "I realized that I still had such a wonderful friend like Jim. Then, the tears came out" (*HB*, 112–13). In short, Tsutsui transformed Huck into a perfect democratic hero who works hard to help Jim out of slavery and is not plagued by psychological struggles.

At the same time, this democratic but simplified *Huckleberry Finn* retains no trace of Twain's literary art of employing irony to satirize the inhumanity of slavery and racism. This is most clearly shown in the scene where Huck decides to help Jim out of slavery. Of course, Tsutsui's Huck does not need to make the ironical but truly serious decision to "go to hell" in order to help Jim, since he does not share the prejudiced belief that people who help runaway slaves are consigned to "everlasting fire." As a result, it is much easier for him to decide to help Jim out of slavery. Instead of saying, "All right, then, I'll *go* to hell" (*HF*, 272), Tsutsui's Huck says: "All right. I can't let Jim be a slave anymore. Jim is not a slave. He is my friend. I will do whatever I can do to help Jim out of slavery" (*HB*, 180). Although this announcement of equal friendship with Jim perfectly fits the image of Huck as an idealistic democratic hero, it totally misses the irony in Twain's original. Tsutsui also ignored a significant theme of the original: Huck's moral growth during his journey with Jim. Twain's Huck gradually outgrows his prejudices as he comes to recognize Jim's humanity. But Tsutsui's Huck, who is without racial prejudice, does not have any room to grow. While Tsutsui succeeded in transforming Huck into a democratic role model for postwar Japanese children, he failed to represent Twain's literary achievement in this great work.

Although *Huckleberry Finn* was often distorted by translators in this way, it sometimes stimulated the creative energy of postwar Japanese readers. The well-known Japanese juvenile novelist Shin Shikata is one example. He was greatly impressed with *Huckleberry Finn* when he read it while caring for war orphans on Kyushu Island. He wrote: "Whenever I look back to the origin of my decision to become a juvenile novelist, 'homeless Huck Finn' is there. Huck overlaps the images of my orphans, who used to pick pockets, steal, and smoke, but who hated injustice, loved humor, and were full of energy."[29] Although he confessed that he had not been able to write a novel such as *Huckleberry Finn* utilizing his life in poverty with the war orphans, he said he still believed he could do it someday.

Shikata's reading of *Huckleberry Finn* suggests that postwar Japanese, especially the Japanese underclass, felt a strong connection to Huck because of the similarities of their lives. During the occupation era, many Japanese were fascinated with the abundance of America as shown in imported products of popular culture such as the immensely popular comic strip *Blondie,* translations of *Reader's Digest,* and, above all, Hollywood movies. For many Japanese, "[w]hat made America 'great' was that it was so rich."[30] But Japanese who were struggling with shortages of food and other necessities of everyday life could not possibly relate their lives to these images of American abundance. The film critic Tsuneo Hazumi remembered watching Hollywood movies shortly after the war:

29. Shin Shikata, "*Yadonashi Huck* no Nakamatachi no Koto" (On the friends of *Homeless Huck*), 71.

30. Dower, *Embracing Defeat,* 136. John Dower writes, "*Blondie* featured a 'typical' middle-class American family and had an incalculable influence in shaping popular envy of the consumerism and material comforts of American-style 'democracy.'" Dower, *Embracing Defeat,* 252. See also Takita, *Views on American Life,* 219–33. The Japanese edition of *Reader's Digest* acquired an enormous readership during the occupation. In June 1949, 1,516,000 copies were sold, breaking the record of Japanese magazines. Japanese readers were particularly fascinated with the magazine's series "America Seikatsu no Samazama" (American ways of life), which featured dreamlike images of American consumer culture. Taketoshi Yamamoto, *Senryoki Media Bunseki* (Media analysis of the occupation era), 506, 515.

> First-run theaters were damaged by air raids and they were turned into temporary shacks with leaks in the roofs, but the American movies we saw there showed the images of dreams unimaginable in our country. . . . Everything looked like the world of dreams which we forgot a long time ago. What a great gap between American movies . . . and our present lives. We, the people of worldly minds, used to walk into town immediately after the war to watch extravagant American feasts on the silver screen with our stomachs growling.[31]

For these people, Huck's harsh world was more familiar than the world of abundance in Hollywood movies. As Shikata's reading of *Huckleberry Finn* demonstrates, Huck gave hope and courage to postwar Japanese by showing that a person with a large heart can sustain both humanity and friendship despite poor and miserable living conditions. It was not only Japanese translators but also readers who read, interpreted, and assimilated *Huckleberry Finn* in terms of their own cultural and social experiences in postwar Japan.

Japanese juvenile translators, then, saw Tom and Huck as democratic heroes who resonated with the social and cultural climate of postwar Japan. At the same time, because Tom and Huck were regarded as juvenile delinquents who might have a bad influence on Japanese children, they were also transformed into genteel figures.

The divided image of Tom and Huck, who were seen as both idealistic democratic heroes and dangerous juvenile delinquents, mirrored the Japanese people's contradictory views on the transformation of their society under American democratization. As we have seen, the Japanese welcomed both freedom and democracy after experiencing the tyrannical oppression of the wartime imperial government. At the same time, however, many Japanese were worried about moral confusion resulting from excessive freedom. A variety of educators and critics, for instance, criticized the newly liberated sexual expressions in films and the so-called "decadent" literature that flourished immediately after the war.[32] The mood of the Japanese people therefore swung between high expectations for democracy and apprehensions about excessive freedom. In addition, because the translations of *Tom Sawyer*

31. Quoted in Tanigawa, *American Films and Occupation Policy,* 12.
32. Hirano, *Mr. Smith Goes to Tokyo,* 157; Dower, *Embracing Defeat,* 161–62.

and *Huckleberry Finn* were mainly for children, it is understandable that Japanese adults overreacted when it came to the influences of these books. In short, the Japanese people, who were experiencing drastic transformations of their world after the war, entailing dramatic changes in their nation's value system, did not feel stable enough to accept Tom and Huck as they are. Japanese children still had to wait to encounter Tom and Huck as English-language readers knew them.[33]

The reformation of the nationalistic and militaristic education system was one of the main goals of the postwar democratization of Japanese society. Historian John Dower writes that under the leadership of the CI&E, the Japanese Ministry of Education was "transformed into one of the country's most systematic and zealous proponents of 'peace and democracy.'" One year after the end of the war, the ministry issued the Shin Kyoiku Shishin (New Educational Guidance) act to help construct "a democratic, peaceful nation of culture." The Japanese government took a totalitarian approach to the democratization of education. For instance, it ordered all militaristic and nationalistic passages in existing school textbooks to be systematically erased with brush and ink and distributed new textbooks called *Shonen Shojo no tame no Minshu Tokuhon* (Democracy readers for boys and girls).[34] Mark Twain's works, rich in democratic humor and humanistic messages, naturally caught the eye of those who were trying to free Japanese textbooks from didacticism and authoritarianism. In contrast to the absence of Twain in prewar and wartime Japanese textbooks, his works appeared frequently in postwar textbooks.[35]

Undoubtedly, Twain's humor was one of the main reasons for his

33. Some scholars and critics did object to juvenile translations that were unfaithful to the originals. See Hitoshi Ishida, "Distorted Translations of *Tom Sawyer*"; Fukuda, "Three Translations of *Uncle Tom's Cabin*," 22–25; Sekino et al., "Problems in the Books of Juvenile Translations," 9–14. As a result of these criticisms, Iwanami Shoten started the Iwanami Shonen Bunko (Iwanami juvenile paperback) series in 1950 to provide faithful translations. *Tom Sawyer no Boken,* a translation by popular children's novelist Momoko Ishii, was published in this series in 1952.

34. Dower, *Embracing Defeat,* 247–49; Shigetoshi Shinohara, *Shonen Shojo no tame no Minshu Tokuhon.*

35. See the section of the bibliography titled "Mark Twain and His Works in Japanese School Textbooks."

inclusion in Japanese textbooks. At the end of the war, the element of humor was almost entirely missing from school textbooks. Militaristic nationalism had become dominant in textbooks under the strict wartime censorship by the Japanese government.[36] Although humorous stories, stories about America and American heroes, and translations of English and American literature sometimes appeared in textbooks before the war, they almost completely disappeared from wartime school textbooks. In their place were idealized war stories and nationalistic essays such as "Marai wo Susumu" (March in Malaya), "Singapore no Kanraku" (The fall of Singapore), and "Kokugo no Chikara" (Power of national language).[37] For the purpose of liberating textbooks from this grave tradition of fanatic nationalism, humorous stories by and about Twain were ideal. In addition, since many Japanese considered America their democratic model, a representative American writer such as Twain was a welcome addition to textbooks.

However, Twain did not deserve all the credit for his popularity in Japanese textbooks. A large part of it belonged to Kyukin Susukida, a well-known humorist and essayist. Many of the short stories by and about Twain that appeared in the textbooks were reprinted from Susukida's *Chabanashi* (Chitchat over tea) books, a series of best-selling collections of humorous pieces.[38] One of these pieces, "Enzetsu wo Nusumareta Hanashi" (A stolen speech), appeared in at least three dif-

36. See Saburo Kuwabara, *Shonen Kurabu no Koro: Showa Zenki no Jido Bungaku* (Around the time of *Shonen Kurabu*: Juvenile literature in the first half of the Showa era), 251–76.

37. Stories about Lincoln, Washington, and Edison; translations of Shakespeare's works; and *warai-banashi* (humorous tales) appeared in prewar elementary school textbooks on ethics and language but were not included in textbooks from 1941 to 1945. See Kokuritsu Kyouiku Kenkyujo Fuzoku Kyouiku Toshokan, ed., *Kokutei Kyokasho Naiyo Sakuin, Jinjo-ka Shushin Kokugo Shoka Hen: Kokutei Kyokasho Naiyo no Hensen* (Index of government-approved textbooks, elementary school course ethics, national language, songs: Transformation of textbook contents). For "Marai wo Susumu," "Singapore no Kanraku," and "Kokugo no Chikara," see *Shotoka Kokugo 8* (Elementary school national language; Tokyo: Monbusho, 1943), 101–6, 116–18, and 141–45, respectively.

38. Kyukin Susukida (1877–1945) started his career as a poet but moved into journalism. He edited the literary section of *Osaka Mainichi Newspaper,* and *Chabanashi* (1916) was a collection of essays that originally appeared in the editor's column. The following books in the series were *Nochi no Chabanashi* (Chitchat over tea, continued; 1918) and *Shin Chabanashi* (New chitchat over tea; 1919); an omnibus edition, *Chabanashi Zenshu* (Complete chitchat over tea), was pub-

ferent postwar school textbooks. In this story, Twain and his friend Chauncey Depew are asked to deliver speeches at a dinner. Twain goes first, and his speech is so humorous and successful that Depew finds it almost impossible to follow. When Depew's turn comes, he stands up and says with perfect composure that he and Twain exchanged the manuscripts of their speeches in advance and that he in fact wrote the speech that Twain has just delivered. Adding that he has unfortunately lost the manuscript Twain wrote for him, he calmly returns to his seat without giving a speech. The audience loudly applauds Depew's wit and Twain realizes he has been outsmarted by his friend. After the dinner, a man who naively believed Depew's words approaches Twain and assures him that the speech he delivered was truly boring. Twain, of course, is greatly put out by this comment.[39]

This story would not have been publishable in the didactic prewar and wartime Japanese school textbooks, which were void of humor. How could readers find moral ethics in this humorous episode? The episode, about a man who succeeds not by honest effort but by his sense of humor and inspirational wit, seems to ridicule the prewar and wartime conventional moral ethics of hard work and honesty. It might be said that the elements of antididacticism and humor in this short piece were the main reasons why it was welcomed in postwar Japan during the democratic liberation of Japanese education from prewar and wartime traditionalism. The story was published in various postwar language textbooks for seventh graders for almost twenty years until the early 1960s and must have influenced the image of Mark Twain for millions of postwar Japanese.

Elements of humor were also emphasized in introducing Twain's own works in textbooks. One 1954 textbook introduced *Tom Sawyer* by explaining the reason for studying humorous stories:

> Imagine a life without laughter. In the streets, in school, and at home, all the people have indifferent and expressionless faces. . . . This is truly unbearable. If you just think of it, you can easily understand the role of

---

lished in 1924. The humorous stories of Susukida and Kuni Sasaki found an appreciative audience in the liberal atmosphere of the Taisho democracy.

39. Kyukin Susukida, "Enzetsu wo Nusumareta Hanashi" (A stolen speech), in *Shin Chugaku Kokugo 1* (1952, 1954) and *Chugakko Kokugo 1-nen* (1962). See appendix, "Twain and His Works in Japanese School Textbooks."

> laughter in life. There are many kinds of laughter. There is not only innocent, cheerful laughter but also evil, detestable laughter. It is humor that encourages this innocent, cheerful laughter and softens people's hearts. We would like to become people who have a sense of humor. We also hope to make this world a better place by nurturing laughter that is as healthy as possible.[40]

Of course, this emphasis on humor would have been unimaginable in wartime textbooks, with their fanatic nationalism.

In the same textbook, two well-known episodes from *Tom Sawyer* were introduced under the title "Jam to Kabutomushi" (Jam and beetle). The first episode is the opening scene of the book, in which Tom, having eaten jam on the sly, succeeds in escaping Aunt Polly's whip. The second episode, from chapter 5, is about Tom's mischief at a church service. Bored with the sermon, Tom starts playing with his "pinchbug." When a curious dog approaches the bug and is bitten, it yelps in agony and runs through the church, interrupting the solemn service. Although the congregation tries hard to suppress its laughter, it is clearly entertained by the incident. Tom feels good about having provided some relief for people who were also bored with the service.[41]

Needless to say, both excerpts succeeded in accomplishing the goal of introducing humor to students. More importantly, they were not only humorous but also democratic and antiauthoritarian. In both episodes, humor is employed in order to describe Tom's disobedience to authority figures and institutions, such as Aunt Polly, the preacher, and the church. Like Susukida's piece on the stolen speech, these pieces would have been unpublishable in prewar and wartime textbooks, which were void of humor and emphasized obedience to elders and authorities. In the era of democratization, however, they were a means to liberate Japanese children from the grave traditions of the past.

Of Twain's major works, the one that most frequently appeared in postwar Japanese textbooks was the famous whitewashing episode in chapter 2 of *The Adventures of Tom Sawyer*.[42] In this chapter, Aunt

40. Kunio Yanagita, ed., *Atarashii Kokugo Chugaku 3-nen* (New national language, 9th grade), 1:120.

41. Eiji Ishida, trans., "Jam to Kabutomushi."

42. See apppendix for Natsuya Mitsuyoshi's and Eiji Ishida's translations, both from 1951, and Kinetaro Yoshida's 1957 translation, all of which were titled "Hei wo Nuru Tom Sawyer" (Tom Sawyer whitewashing the wall).

Polly punishes Tom by making him whitewash a fence on a Saturday. By pretending to enjoy the chore, he makes it look so attractive that his friends beg him for turns at it themselves. They even pay him for the privilege. Tom discovers, as Twain puts it, "that Work consists of whatever a body is *obliged* to do, and that Play consists of whatever a body is not obliged to do" (*TS*, 32). He also gets the fence painted without working at it himself, thereby deceiving his aunt.

This episode must have been truly detestable to prewar and wartime educators, who highly valued children's honest work and obedience to their elders. Postwar educators, however, saw the episode as an instructive example of how to break down traditional authoritarianism and as a demonstration of the effectiveness of democratic ways of thinking. One textbook introduced the story as follows: "The significant wisdom of human life is not always found in difficult books and grave morals. Instead, truly important wisdom is hidden in our daily lives. Look at the case of Tom, who was ordered to whitewash the fence on Saturday. As he tries to escape from the work, he gradually realizes the true meaning of work."[43] The idea underlying this brief introduction is both antiauthoritarian and democratic: Tom is portrayed as a democratic figure who acquires his individual philosophy through the experience of everyday life, not through authoritative books or moral teachings. Such idealization of Tom was common in the postwar era.

As we have seen, America was a model for many Japanese educators in the democratization movement. Stories favorable to American life started appearing in Japanese textbooks within several years after the end of the war. Stories by Japanese who had studied in America introduced themes of American friendship and egalitarianism. One textbook featured a piece about Jo Niijima, who founded Doshisha University in Kyoto with the help of American Christians.[44] CI&E encouraged Japanese educators to rewrite textbooks using American models. A number of American textbooks and references were donated to "designated 'textbook centers' for local use of Japan's educational authorities, teachers, scholars, and everyone involved in the production of

43. Seijo Kokubungakkai, ed., *Chugaku Gendai Kokugo 2* (Junior high school modern national language 2,) 1:100.

44. See Shiho Sakanishi, "Aisareru Shojo" (A girl loved); "Meguriai" (Encounter), in *Kokugo Dai 6 Gakunen* (National language, sixth grade; Tokyo: Tokyo Shoseki, 1948), 2:43–76.

new educational materials for Japan."[45] The popularity of the whitewashing episode in *Tom Sawyer* was a result of the Americanization of Japanese textbooks. Just a few years after the end of the war, the episode appeared in *Shonen Hyakka,* the Japanese version of *The Book of Knowledge,* a popular American educational magazine of the time. Some Japanese textbooks copied the episode word for word from the magazine, and one even duplicated the magazine's list of study questions without any alteration.[46] The Japanese version of *The Book of Knowledge* was a by-product of the country's fascination with America. Its publisher, Nichi-Bei Shuppan Sha (Japan-US Publishing Company), called it "the biggest American juvenile magazine," and claimed that "75 percent of American model families let their children read *The Book of Knowledge.*"[47] Japanese educators, eager to assimilate American educational values, dutifully copied the whitewashing episode word for word.

Although educators emphasized Twain's humor and antiauthoritarianism, they did not ignore ethics in adapting his stories for textbooks. The whitewashing episode, for instance, was taught as a moral tale in Japanese classrooms. Textbooks quoted Twain's explanation of why whitewashing was not recognized as a tiring chore by Tom's friends: "Work consists of whatever a body is obliged to do, and Play consists of whatever a body is not obliged to do." This is the message that Japanese educators stressed. For example, Japanese textbooks asked similar questions about this story, such as: "What kind of attitude should we take to a difficult but necessary task to do? Think about it, examining Tom's experience in this story."[48] Some students, impressed with Tom's shrewd scheme, might have answered, "We should pretend to enjoy a difficult task and attract foolish people to do it instead." This answer, which is selfish but true to Tom Sawyer's mind, would have been objected to by schoolteachers. The model answer would have been:

45. "Thirteen Sets of Sample Texts and Reference Books Available for Use in Rewriting of Textbooks for Japan's Schools," *CI&E Bulletin,* November 4, 1947, 7.

46. Mitsuyoshi, "Tom Sawyer Whitewashing the Wall," in *Shonen Hyakka* 1 (January 1949), 40–46. For the copied list of questions, see Sanseido Henshujo, ed., *Chugaku Shin Kokugo 1,* 1:116–17.

47. *Shonen Hyakka,* 61.

48. Kokubungakkai, *Chugaku Gendai Kokugo 2,* 1:108.

"We should avoid perceiving work as what we are obliged to do, and work on difficult tasks as if we enjoy them." Despite Japanese educators' interpretation of this episode as a moral tale, Twain seems rather to enjoy portraying the pathos of human nature, which can so easily be deceived. This was perhaps considered not educational enough to merit publication in a textbook, so the story was framed as a moral tale in accordance with the deep-seated didacticism of Japanese classrooms.

Adventures of Huckleberry Finn was excerpted in only one of the postwar textbooks. Most of the stories discussed here appeared in textbooks for seventh graders. However, even in translation, *Huckleberry Finn* was too difficult for the average seventh grader to digest. An excerpt appeared instead in a 1959 language textbook for ninth graders, side by side with a selection from Romain Rolland's *Jean Christoph.*[49] Except for a few brief references, this was the first and last appearance of *Huckleberry Finn* in a Japanese textbook. The textbook presented the scene in chapter 16 in which Huck and Jim are looking for Cairo, a village located at the junction of the Mississippi and Ohio Rivers. They plan to leave the raft there and canoe up the Ohio to the free states in the North. As their prospects of finding Cairo increase, Huck feels guilty about helping Jim escape from his owner. Nearly defeated by his conscience, Huck decides to report Jim as a runaway and takes his canoe to the shore. When two slave hunters approach and question him, however, he cannot bring himself to turn Jim in and tells them a lie instead (*HF,* 121–29).

The Japanese educators who selected this episode for the textbook seem to have been aware of both the greatness and significance of *Adventures of Huckleberry Finn.* In the accompanying teacher's manual, they explained that *Huckleberry Finn* "is recognized as one of the world classics that all people have to read at least once, and its humanism will provide a great model for the development of humanity among our students."[50] Unfortunately, however, their understanding of *Huckleberry Finn* was superficial. The textbook version omitted

49. Naotaro Tatsunokuchi, trans., "Huckleberry to Jim" (Huckleberry and Jim).

50. *Kairyudo Kokugo Sogo 3 Ge, Kyoushiyo Shidosho* (Kairyudo general national language 3, teacher's manual; Tokyo: Kairyudo, 1959), 21.

significant aspects of the original. For instance, in accordance with the genteel tradition of Japanese translation, Huck's colloquial language was again mostly lost. The textbook's Huck never speaks ungrammatically and seldom uses slang or colloquial expressions. This "improvement" of Huck's language was not a result of the translator's consideration for its publication in a school textbook. The excerpt was taken from the above-mentioned book *Adventures of Huckleberry Finn: An American Boy Who Sought Freedom,* translated by Naotaro Tatsunokuchi and published ten years earlier, with language equally grammatical and standard.[51]

As noted in the teacher's manual, however, the passage was "translated specifically for junior high school students," and alterations were indeed made to bring the text into accordance with the ingrained conservatism of Japanese textbooks.[52] For example, Tatsunokuchi softened some of Huck's racist views and expressions for the textbook adaptation. In Twain's original, Huck is shocked to hear Jim say that he would send an "Ab'litionist" to "steal" his wife and children when he became free. Huck says, "It was according to the old saying, 'give a nigger an inch and he'll take an ell.' Thinks I, this is what comes of my not thinking" (*HF,* 124). In Tatsunokuchi's original translation, he faithfully translated the word *nigger* as *kuronbo,* which also has a strong racist connotation. In the textbook adaptation, though, he changed *kuronbo* to *kokujin,* a neutral term meaning "blacks." In Twain's original, Huck continues: "Here was this nigger which I had as good as helped to run away, coming right out flat-footed and saying he would steal his children—children that belonged to a man I didn't even know; a man that hadn't ever done me no harm. I was sorry to hear Jim say that, it was such a lowering of him" (*HF,* 124). In his original translation, Tatsunokuchi faithfully translated these lines, which demonstrate Huck's racist understanding of Jim.[53] However, they were deleted in the textbook adaptation.

Although it is impossible to fully explain the reasons for these alterations, one of them seems to have been the Ministry of Education's censorship of textbooks. Although the ministry avoided the term *ken'e-*

51. Tatsunokuchi, trans., *Huckleberry Finn no Boken.*
52. Kairyudo general national language 3, teacher's manual, 59.
53. Tatsunokuchi, *Adventures of Huckleberry Finn,* 127–28.

tsu (censorship), preferring to describe its function as *kentei* (approval), it was engaged in absolute censorship. As a result, Japanese history textbooks were not able to make clear references toward unflattering chapters in the country's history until recently.[54] Japanese students therefore did not learn from their textbooks certain facts about World War II, such as the massacres in East and Southeast Asia and the treatment of Korean *jugun ianfu* (comfort women) who were forced to serve the Japanese military. The ministry also censored literary works chosen for publication in language textbooks, sometimes revealing an obtuse understanding of creative writing. A poem in the *kansai* (western regional) dialect was rendered in standard Japanese for publication in textbooks, thus losing the lively colloquial expressions of the original.[55] Similar examples of suppression abound. In the same year that Tatsunokuchi's *Huckleberry Finn* appeared in a textbook, a Japanese work of fiction was denied inclusion in a language textbook because it had a "dangerous scene of tree-climbing." Literary works containing descriptions of poverty and scenes of fighting were also frequently censored. One story was suppressed just because it was about a child with a single parent. Translations of Western juvenile classics were not exempt from government textbook censorship. The Italian writer Edmondo De Amicis's *Cuore* was prohibited because "it employs a disabled boy as a main character."[56] No wonder Huck's slang and colloquial expressions were unacceptable in Japanese textbooks. Or that *Huckleberry Finn* disappeared from Japanese textbooks after its single appearance in 1959 and that other episodes, with their descriptions of violence, never appeared at all. In contrast to the relatively harmless *Tom Sawyer,* which appeared for nearly twenty years in a variety of postwar textbooks, *Huckleberry Finn* was too wild and controversial to be accepted by the government's genteel censors and educators.

54. Saburo Ienaga, a leading Japanese historian, fought the government censorship of history textbooks, arguing that the Ministry of Education's actions were unconstitutional. His thirty-two-year lawsuit ended in 1997 when the Supreme Court approved the current system of government textbook censorship.

55. Yoshitomo Imae, "Nihongo to Jido Bungaku" (Japanese language and juvenile literature; 1974), 73–76.

56. Sueyoshi Eguchi, "Kyokasho Shuppan no Jiyu ni Tsuite" (On the freedom of textbook publication; 1970), 19–20.

Even in the classrooms where *Huckleberry Finn* was taught, understanding of this American classic was limited. In particular, the significance of Jim was neglected. In the textbook in which Tatsunokuchi's translation appeared, the questions following the story include: "What are the personalities of Huck and Jim? How are their personalities represented in this story?" In the teacher's manual, the answer to this question is: "Huck Finn is a person of humanity and sincerity. Because of his humane qualities, Huck could not help protecting Jim from slave hunters." In contrast with its high estimation of Huck, the manual is very critical of Jim: "Jim . . . is a man of naive and simplistic personality who minds only his own business."[57] This answer ignores the possibility of reading Jim as someone with a complex personality. Even in the episode reprinted in the textbook, Jim can be read not as a naive runaway slave but as a shrewd man who foresees the effect of his words on Huck and manipulates him to gain his freedom. For instance, just after Huck makes up his mind to report Jim and is preparing to paddle his canoe to the shore, Jim says to him, "Jim won't ever forgit you, Huck; you's de bes' fren' Jim's ever had; en you's de *only* fren' ole Jim's got now." As Huck makes his way across the river, Jim shouts, "Dah you goes, de ole true Huck; de on'y white genlman dat ever kep' his promise to ole Jim" (*HF*, 124). Readers can choose to interpret Jim's words as his honest and innocent expression of gratitude. However, we can also read them as Jim's shrewd attempt to use this moment to remind Huck of their friendship. We can be open to the possibility that Jim is a perceptive character who senses that Huck is planning to turn him in and that he speaks the words above in the hope of discouraging Huck from betraying him.[58] In fact, it is unlikely that an attentive reader of the entire novel would view Jim as a person "who minds only his own business." Twain depicted Jim not as a sim-

57. Kagejiro Kazamaki, ed., *Kokugo Sogo 3,* 2:44; *Kairyudo General National Language 3, Teacher's Manual,* 63.

58. A similar reading of Jim can be found in Ralph Wiley's unproduced screenplay for the director Spike Lee. See Shelley Fisher Fishkin, "In Praise of 'Spike Lee's Huckleberry Finn' by Ralph Wiley." See also Fishkin's insightful essay about the emergence of new views on Jim in the 1990s, in which she discusses various critics' interpretations of Jim as a perceptive, independent character under the "mask" of minstrelsy. Shelley Fisher Fishkin, "New Perspectives on 'Jim' in the 1990s."

plistic, selfish person but as a man of deep sorrow who always cares about other people. Jim is not only a caring father who cries for his family but also an unselfish person who, in the final chapters, is willing to jeopardize his freedom in order to save Tom Sawyer's life.

There may have been Japanese teachers who simply ignored the superficial understanding of Jim in the teacher's manual and encouraged students' creative readings of him. Those who blindly followed the manual would have forced on their students a negative image of Jim that is truly different from the character Twain depicted. As discussed in chapter 1, the characterization of blacks as good-hearted, simple people was common in popular cultural texts, not only in America but also in Japan until recently. The simplistic characterization of Jim in the textbook probably reflected deep-seated prejudices against the black race among the Japanese.

Thus, Twain and his works appeared in postwar Japanese textbooks in a variety of ways. His American humor was appreciated at a time of democratization of Japanese education. Twain surely provided a model for Japanese educators who sought to overcome the traditional didacticism of prewar and wartime textbooks. At the same time, those educators were not liberal enough to adapt Twain's works faithfully. Their conservatism led them to transform those works into genteel, didactic stories. As seen in the case of the textbook adaptation of *Huckleberry Finn,* Japanese educators' concern with making the intended effect on students often outweighed their respect for Twain's literary art.

Despite this disrespect, Twain and his works, albeit in bowdlerized form, were shared in Japan on an unprecedented scale as a result of their appearance in school textbooks. Although Twain's presence in Japanese classrooms was still limited compared to the prevalence of his works in American classrooms, his popularity in postwar Japan was truly surprising considering the absolute disregard of Twain in prewar and wartime Japan.

Unfortunately, however, Twain gradually disappeared from Japanese textbooks. Although *Tom Sawyer* and *Huckleberry Finn* were included on recommended reading lists in textbooks through the early 1960s, Twain and his works almost completely disappeared from Japanese textbooks in the years that followed. The reasons behind this disappearance are not immediately apparent. American literature was continuously popular in textbooks for the rest of the twentieth century. Other American writers such as Hemingway, Pearl Buck, Harriet Beecher Stowe, and O. Henry frequently appeared even after the postwar boom of American literature and culture.[59] It can be argued that, as the democratic and liberal atmosphere of postwar Japanese education receded, Twain's works were considered too "humorous" to be employed in textbooks. It might also be true that in light of Japanese educators' shallow understanding of *Huckleberry Finn,* Twain's works were seen as merely average juvenile literature, without depth or serious issues for students to study.

Even though Twain virtually vanished from Japanese school textbooks in the 1960s, his works obtained their greatest popularity in Japan over the next two decades in a medium that was considerably different. It was animation that had the greatest impact on Japanese perceptions of Twain's works in the 1970s and '80s.

59. After the late 1960s, Twain's works do not appear in the content list of junior high school language textbooks. Kokuritsu Kyouiku Kenkyujo Fuzoku Kyoiku Toshokan and Kyokasho Kenkyu Center, ed., *Chugakko Kokugo Kyokasho Naiyo Sakuin* (Index for the contents of junior high school national language textbooks). For the frequent appearance of American writers, see the same content list. It should be noted that Twain's works were also ignored in postwar high school textbooks. Gen'ichiro Fukawa, "Kouto Gakko Kokugoka Kyokasho Database Ichiran, 1950–1994" (Content list of high school national language textbooks, 1950–1994), presented at the 89th annual meeting of Zenkoku Daigaku Kokugo Kyoiku Gakkai (Association for national language education at universities), Shizuoka, Japan.

4

Japanese Animations of *Huckleberry Finn* and *Tom Sawyer*

Animation (*anime* in Japanese) is one of the most significant popular cultural genres in late twentieth-century Japan. As critics have suggested, anime and manga (Japanese comic strips and graphic novels) replaced literature as the major form of narrative entertainment for children in the 1970s and '80s. In contrast with the dramatic increase in popularity of anime and manga, children's literature had fewer and fewer readers after the late 1970s. Although proponents of juvenile literature have warned that a reliance on visual images limits children's imaginations, the popularity of anime and manga has not decreased. In 1980, ten animes were shown each day by the major television networks, two-thirds of which enjoyed audience ratings above 20 percent. In a 1995 survey, anime was the most popular genre of television programs among children.[1]

1. See Hiroshi Sunada, "'Eizo' ga Tsukuru 'Monogatari' to 'Kotoba' ga Tsukuru 'Monogatari'" (A story made by images and a story made by words), 14–16; Yasuyoshi Sekiguchi, "Nihon Jido Bungaku no Seiritsu: Shisoshi Shakaishi no

Anime is not only for children, however. Many adults are devoted fans. Anime fan clubs and Web discussion groups whose members are mainly grownups are flourishing all over the country. Anime takes in a wide variety of genres, answering a variety of demands among grown-up viewers. Susan J. Napier, a leading anime scholar, says, "[A]nime works include everything that Western audiences are accustomed to seeing in live-action films." There are anime films in the genres of romance, comedy, tragedy, adventure, psychodrama, and even pornography. Transcending both age and genre limitations, anime has succeeded in attracting immense audiences. Hayao Miyazaki's *Mononoke Hime* (Princess Mononoke) was a social phenomenon in 1997, setting new box-office records for Japanese theatrical feature films. Miyazaki had an even greater success in 2001 with *Sen to Chihiro no Kamikakushi* (Sen and Chihiro spirited away; released in the United States as *Spirited Away*). In 1999, half the tickets sold in Japan for Japanese feature films were for animated films.[2]

Considering the popularity and diversity of anime since the 1970s, it seems natural that *Tom Sawyer* and *Huckleberry Finn,* two of the best-known American classics in Japan, have been repeatedly adapted as animes. The anime versions of these books provide good examples for demonstrating the ways in which products of American culture are transformed to fit into cultures outside of America. This chapter will examine three Japanese television anime productions of *Huckleberry Finn* and *Tom Sawyer* and the ways in which they transformed Twain's originals in terms of race, gender, didacticism, and gentility.

Inevitably, the discussion at times will be very critical, since the anime versions utterly neglect significant elements of Twain's originals. However, the adaptations should not be denounced outright just because they are unfaithful. As Robert Stam writes, "[O]ur statements about films based on novels or other sources need to be less moralistic, less panicked, less implicated in unacknowledged hierarchies, more rooted in contextual and intertexual history. Above all, we need to be

---

Shiten kara" (The formation of Japanese juvenile literature: In terms of intellectual and social history), 42; Kunimatsu, "Waiting for a Dirtier Tom Sawyer," 45; Choko Hatakeyama, "'Monogatari Kankyo' toshite no Televi Animation" (Televised animation as a narrative environment), 29.

2. Napier, *Anime from* Akira *to* Princess Mononoke, 6–7.

less concerned with inchoate notions of 'fidelity' and to give more attention to dialogical responses—to readings, critiques, interpretations, and rewritings of prior material."[3] Twain's works and their anime adaptations were created in different eras, different nations, and different media, and it is necessary to consider those differences in order to explain the animes' alterations of the originals. Therefore, this chapter will consider various cultural discourses behind the anime adaptations, such as the changing Japanese perceptions of women and blacks and the changing trends in anime television series.

Huckleberry Finn no Boken (Adventures of Huckleberry Finn) was the first anime adaptation of a work by Twain. Twenty-six weekly episodes were produced by Group Tack and aired on the Fuji Television Network from January 1 to June 25, 1976. At a total length of nearly twelve hours, it is undoubtedly one of the longest visual adaptations of *Huckleberry Finn* in any country.

This first Twain anime followed the contemporary trend of television anime. In the 1970s and '80s, Japan experienced a boom of meisaku anime (world classic anime) series based on classics of juvenile literature such as Andersen's fairy tales, Johanna Spyri's *Heidi,* Sterling North's *Rascal,* De Amicis's *Cuore,* Alcott's *Little Women,* Ouida's *A Dog of Flanders,* and Lucy Maud Montgomery's *Anne of Green Gables.* These series were well suited to the distinctive features of anime. In contrast to American animations and comics, which traditionally depict characters through lively action and movement, anime and manga excel at the subtle expression of characters' inner thoughts, using fewer actions. Lynn Johnston, the Canadian author of the comic strip *For Better or for Worse,* says: "Japanese manga characters express things through their eyes. But American and our comics heavily rely on body language. We express characters' feelings through their exaggerated physical movement and gestures."[4] Works of literature, which deal more with

3. Robert Stam, "Beyond Fidelity," 75–76.

4. Zen Enoki, president of Enoki Films, interview by author, August 28, 2002, Tokyo; Andrew Pollack, "Japan, a Superpower among Superheroes," *New York Times,* September 17, 1995, sec. 2, 32; Johnston quoted in Kosei Ono, "Manga to Anime Nihon to Obei no Sogo Shinto: Ekkyou Suru Subculture" (The mutual penetration of comics and anime between Japan and the West: Subculture crossing the border), 260.

characters' inner thoughts than with exaggerated actions, are a perfect fit for the conventions of manga and anime.

Zuiyo Enterprises produced the earliest meisaku anime series in the early 1970s, and its successor, Nippon Animation Company, produced numerous series from 1975 until 1997. The series were shown on a program called *Sekai Meisaku Anime Gekijo* (World classic theater), also known as *Calpis Gekijo* (Calpis theater) after the soft drink company that was its sole sponsor until 1979. During the golden age of meisaku anime in the 1970s and '80s, Nippon Animation won government awards for excellent juvenile television almost every year and average viewer ratings were above 20 percent; the highest were around 30 percent, which was truly high in Japanese television.[5] Although contemporary authors of children's literature lamented readers' indifference toward their works, meisaku anime received a remarkable response from the public. For instance, as the final episode of *A Dog of Flanders* approached, newspapers and the television network received thousands of letters from viewers who begged the series' producers to avoid the tragic ending of Ouida's original story. Japanese tourists traveled to Antwerp in search of the actual locales of *Heidi.* Their frequent inquiries led city officials to erect a statue of Heidi in the center of the city. Meisaku animes were also shown on Asian and European television, drawing millions of global viewers. Portugal even held a Heidi look-alike contest modeled after the character in the Japanese anime.[6]

Huckleberry Finn no Boken appeared at the height of meisaku anime's popularity in Japan. Like the other series, it was broadcast by the Fuji Television Network and its time slot, aimed at family viewers, was Sunday dinnertime. Introduced in a newspaper as "one of the animes that are in line with the meisaku anime trend based on foreign children's literature," this first *Huckleberry Finn* anime was planned to be

5. Average ratings of series in the 1970s were: *A Dog of Flanders,* 22.7 percent, *Heidi,* 20.8 percent, *Cuore,* 21.8 percent, *Rascal,* 23.1 percent. The highest rating for *A Dog of Flanders* was 30.1 percent. Junzo Nakajima, executive producer of Nippon Animation, e-mail to the author, December 19, 2002.

6. Masashi Matsumoto, *20-seiki Televi Tokuhon, Sekai Meisaku Gekijo Taizen* (Twentieth-century television readers: Everything on *World Classic Theater*), 13, 249.

faithful to Twain's original. The outline of each episode in the original proposal shows no considerable alteration from the book.[7] But some alterations were made during production. For instance, Tom Sawyer was completely eliminated. The series starts with a gang of boys hunting for treasure and, instead of Tom, Huck is their leader. Impressed with Huck's courage and kindness, the other boys respect his decisions (*HFB*, episodes 1, 2). The elimination of Tom Sawyer allowed the filmmakers to focus on the relationship between Huck and Jim without being distracted by Tom's childish schemes. As a result, the controversial ending of the original, in which Tom Sawyer dominates the story, is significantly different in the anime. In contrast to Tom, with his fantastic and cruel scheme to free Jim, Huck helps Jim to escape with no delay (*HFB*, episode 25).

In the anime, Huck is portrayed as a more active and aggressive character. Although it is unimaginable in the original, he fights back against his violent father, biting him on the arm (*HFB*, episode 4). He also punches a boy in the nose for making racist comments (*HFB*, episode 20). In this way he is quite different from Twain's Huck, who is not an aggressive fighter at all but rather a somewhat passive character who tends to avoid trouble. It is hard to imagine Twain's Huck being welcomed by juvenile anime viewers, who tend to prefer courageous, superman-type heroes. The images of an aggressive Huck in *Huckleberry Finn no Boken* perfectly match this image of a hero.

In the anime, Huck is sometimes excessively aggressive. The scene of the lynching of the King and Duke is one example. Twain's Huck, disgusted with the lynch mob, says: "Well, it made me sick to see it; and I was sorry for them poor pitiful rascals, it seemed like I couldn't feel any hardness against them any more in the world. It was a dreadful thing to see. Human beings *can* be awful cruel to one another" (*HF*, 291). The anime could not be more different. Surprisingly, Huck himself is a member of the mob. The narrator explains: "Huck thought that it served them right. . . . But, when he thought of Jim who was sold by them, he started feeling that this punishment is not enough for

7. "Shin-bangumi, Huckleberry Finn no Boken: Akaruku Tanoshii Iyokuteki na Doga" (New program, *Adventures of Huckleberry Finn*: A cheerful, enjoyable, and innovative animation), *Yomiuri Shimbun*, January 1, 1976; "Kikakusho Kogai" (Proposal and summary; see appendix listing for *Huckleberry Finn no Boken*).

them." At this point Huck picks up a stick and hits the King and Duke with it, yelling, "Give Jim back to me! Bastards! Give Jim back to me!" (*HFB*, episode 25). In this way, the anime denies Huck's pacifism and overlooks his critical views about the violent aspects of human nature. The targets of Twain's satire in *Huckleberry Finn* are not only slavery and racism but also the insensitivity of ordinary people who unthinkingly sustain such social habits and institutions as lynching, racism, and slavery. Huck is disgusted with the lynch mob because he intuits that their insensitivity is at the core of social evil. However, the anime turns Huck from a boy who instinctively feels the cruelty of mass hysteria into one who is unaware of it.

Although he is somewhat simplistic in this way, Huck is depicted as a flawless hero of justice and equality. Unlike Twain's Huck, who partly shares the racial prejudice of the antebellum South, the anime's Huck is a straightforward antiracist. In one scene, Jim tries to persuade Huck to return to the Widow Douglas's place and not to get involved in his troubles. Emphasizing the difference between blacks and whites, Jim urges Huck to go back to the sphere where he is supposed to belong: "Huck, look at them, your hand and my hand. My hand stays black even though I wash it again and again. See? We'd better not be together." Huck rejects Jim's argument, shouting, "What's wrong about a black hand! What's special about a white hand, Jim!" (*HFB*, episode 6). This Huck cannot abide unfair treatment of blacks. In the scene referred to above, a boy from a wealthy southern family refuses to apologize to his slave for wrongly suspecting him of stealing his wallet. The boy says to Huck with a contemptuous chuckle, "Apologize to a slave? Are you insane?" Huck becomes furious at these words and punches the boy in the nose, saying, "YOU are insane. Even a slave is a human being. . . . I don't know whether you are the son of a rich family or a mayor. A man who doesn't care about people's minds is a bastard!" (*HFB*, episode 20). There is no trace in this Huck of the racism against blacks that was naturally shared among most whites in the antebellum South. As a result, he does not need to make his famous decision to "go to hell" to help Jim out of slavery. In the anime, Huck decides to help Jim for the sake of their friendship, without any struggles with his conscience (*HFB*, episode 24).

There are several possible reasons for this alteration of Huck's character. As already suggested, the image of Huck as a fighter for equality would have been welcomed by the anime audience, especially juvenile viewers, who tended to favor heroic men of action. Huck's strong awareness of racism is also understandable in terms of the time when the anime was made; news of the civil rights movement had raised Japanese people's awareness of racism against blacks. In addition, the image of an aggressively antiracist Huck in the anime overlapped the image of a democratic Huck that was repeatedly emphasized in juvenile translations during the postwar democratization movement. In particular, the democratic Huck in Keisuke Tsutsui's 1948 translation *Huckleberry no Boken,* discussed in the previous chapter, is quite similar to the Huck in the anime. However, the democratization of Japan had ended more than twenty years before the appearance of the anime, so it would be hard to argue that that movement still had a significant impact on Japanese perceptions of Huck.

More important in understanding the anime's transformation of Huck into an antiracist was Japanese juvenile viewers' unfamiliarity with American history, in particular its history of racism and slavery. The producers, lacking confidence in viewers' knowledge of the background of the story, inserted brief explanations of slavery and racism in the American antebellum South. For example, the narrator explains, "Around one hundred fifty years ago, slavery still remains in the American South, and blacks whose skin is colored differently from whites were sold by whites and forced to work like cows and horses" (*HFB,* episode 5). The producers also included scenes of the whipping of slaves and separation of slave families (*HFB,* episodes 1, 2, 20). Although in this way they succeeded in introducing the realities of American slavery to Japanese viewers, they stopped short at exploring the subtleties. Even a good-hearted person such as Huck would have partly shared the racist views of the majority and accepted slavery as an inevitable social institution. Most southerners thought that to help a runaway slave was one of the greatest sins. An antebellum white southern boy could never have been a straightforward fighter of racism and slavery as he is in the anime. It would have been too challenging for Japanese viewers, especially juvenile viewers, who had no fundamental knowledge of American slavery, to understand the subtle tensions of slaveholding society embodied by Twain's Huck. The producers therefore ignored the complexity of the character and turned him into a clear-cut antiracist and abolitionist.

For Americans, who are obviously more familiar with their own history, it is apparently unimaginable to neglect this significant aspect of *Huckleberry Finn.* No American film adaptation, even though the main audience is children, completely disregards Huck's struggle with his conscience. Even the frequently criticized Disney version (*The Adventures of Huck Finn,* 1993) portrayed Huck's struggle as an antebellum white Southern boy. But a reviewer of the 1988 Japanese version of *Big River,* the Broadway musical based on *Huckleberry Finn,* noticed that Japanese audiences' unfamiliarity with slavery in the antebellum South was an obstacle to their understanding of the show. He wrote, "It might be hard for Japanese to understand that Huck is not necessarily fighting for the emancipation of slaves."[8]

The anime also transformed Jim into a hero with a more straightforward character. As we have seen, Jim was often neglected in Japanese juvenile adaptations of *Huckleberry Finn.* In the very first translation, Kuni Sasaki deleted the scenes in which Jim shows his humanity and love toward his family. In his only appearance in a postwar Japanese textbook, Jim was portrayed as selfish and simplistic. The anime, however, depicted him as a significant character with a strong sense of independence, equality, and the unfairness of a slaveholding society. Jim says to Huck: "You are in a better situation, because you can run away if you want. We slaves will be almost killed if we run away. . . . I envy you, Huck. We cannot behave like you even if we want to" (*HFB,* episode 2). Unlike Twain's reserved Jim, the anime's Jim even expresses his distrust toward the white race. He tells Huck, "Maybe you cannot understand my feelings as a black because you were raised as a white," and later says, "We blacks are always looked down on by whites and called slaves and niggers. . . . You can't understand our feelings as blacks if you weren't born a black" (*HFB,* episodes 19, 20). Although Twain's Jim is excited about the prospect of his freedom and feels deep sorrow over his separation from his family, he never explicitly refers to

8. "Kokujin Haiyu de Butai ni Atsumi" (The play was deepened by the black actor), review of *Big River,* Aoyama Theater, Tokyo, *Asahi Shimbun,* March 1, 1988, evening ed.

the unfairness of slavery or compares his life as a slave with the free life of whites. In the anime, however, Jim seldom suppresses his dissatisfaction over his unfair lot. This version of Jim is, of course, more acceptable than Twain's Jim to juvenile viewers, who prefer uncomplicated, clear-cut characters.

In the anime, Jim is portrayed as a fatherly or big-brother figure. Age hierarchy is strict in Japan in comparison with Western countries and young people are expected to show respect to their elders. As a result, the anime tends to regard Jim, who is much older than Huck, as superior to Huck. For instance, when Jim displays his knowledge about various things, Huck is impressed with Jim as a superior figure in terms of age, saying, "No wonder, you are older than me!" (*HFB*, episode 5). Jim even boldly ignores the racial hierarchy when he thinks it necessary to teach Huck a lesson. This is evident in the episode in which the dense fog and swift current separate Jim and Huck. After they are reunited, Huck insists they were never separated and that Jim must have been dreaming. When Jim realizes that a trick is being played on him, he shames Huck into apologizing (*HF*, 115–21). The anime scenario writer, Mamoru Sasaki, originally followed Twain in adapting this well-known scene. But later, although it was unusual to do so, he went back to the completed scenario to revise this particular scene. In the revised scenario, Jim, furious over the trick, slaps Huck with no warning (*HFB*, episode 14). This version of the scene completely ignores not only Jim's original peace-loving character but also the reality of racial hierarchy in slaveholding society, where it was unacceptable for a black person to slap a white person. Huck's response in the anime is also unrealistic. Twain's Huck hesitates for a while before he can "humble [him]self" and apologize to Jim (*HF*, 121). In the anime, however, Huck does not hesitate but apologizes to Jim immediately. The narrator explains that "Huck feels Jim's seriousness deep inside his heart. Huck thinks it is Jim's expression of both brotherly love and fatherly consideration to him."[9] In the anime, Jim's bold defiance of the racial hierarchy of antebellum America is justified by the application of Japanese patriarchal tradition and age hierarchy.

9. "Tabi no Odoroki" (Surprise in travel), and "Tabi no Odoroki," revised version, 21–22, 24. See appendix listing for *Huckleberry Finn no Boken*.

Although in this way Twain's Jim is turned into a somewhat different person, this anime finally liberated him from the traditional underestimation of his character in Japanese juvenile translations. Clearly, he is not just Huck's sidekick anymore. His liberation seems partly a reflection of the increase in Japanese people's awareness of the progress of blacks in America in the second half of the twentieth century. Although there is no such episode in Twain, the anime has a scene in which Jim is refused service at a restaurant that has a "No Colored" sign (*HFB*, episode 20). It is unlikely that a village establishment in the antebellum South would have felt the need to announce its segregation policy; segregation was so firmly entrenched that it was not necessary in most places to announce it as in late nineteenth and twentieth-century America.[10] The idea for this scene was apparently provided by images of American activists protesting segregated restaurants. The civil rights movement was still relatively recent when *Huckleberry Finn no Boken* was produced, and such incidents were well known by the Japanese public. The impact of the movement was felt across the Pacific and must have contributed to an awareness of race issues, resulting in the emphasis on Jim in the anime as a liberated, independent character.[11]

Pap Finn was also transformed in the anime. Although he is depicted as a violent drunkard, he is more humanized. For instance, he keeps a squirrel as a pet, feeding it regularly and protecting it from dangerous animals. Moreover, he does not attempt to murder Huck as he does in Twain's original. The anime explains the reason behind his degradation: Pap was a "hard-working pioneer" and a "kind, cheerful, good father" when he started out in St. Petersburg, but his financial failure changed him completely (*HFB*, episode 3). Even then, he retains his affection toward his son. He silently apologizes to Huck: "I thought that I could give you a much better life. But once you fall down to the bottom, it is hell. I couldn't crawl up again. Please forgive

10. See Leon Litwack, *Trouble in Mind: Black Southerners in the Age of Jim Crow;* C. Vann Woodward, *The Strange Career of Jim Crow;* John W. Cell, *The Highest Stage of White Supremacy: The Origins of Segregation in South Africa and the American South.*

11. New views of Jim as an independent, perceptive character have emerged recently in American Mark Twain studies. See Fishkin, "New Perspectives on 'Jim.' "

me, Huck" (*HFB,* episode 4). Pap is depicted as a character who embodies the dark side of American frontier history, with its heavy drinking and high risk of failure. Although the anime tends to sentimentalize Pap as an innocent victim, its representation of the harsh realities of frontier life is praiseworthy, since it challenges the uncritical, romanticized image of American frontier life that might otherwise be shared by Japanese viewers.

As a result of the humanization of Pap, the anime's Huck naturally feels some affection toward his father. He cries over the death of Pap and pours whiskey on his grave (*HFB,* episode 6). American film adaptations of *Huckleberry Finn* also emphasize Huck's sorrow over the death of Pap. In most American film versions, Huck not only cries at the news of his father's death but also blames Jim for keeping it secret during their journey. These scenes seem unrealistic, however, since the American films ignore the human side of Pap and depict him as nothing more than a violent child abuser.[12] In this regard, the anime's portrayal of the relationship between Huck and Pap seems more careful and reasonable.

However, it is also true that the anime tends to sentimentalize family relationships. In comparison, Twain's representation of the relationship between Huck and Pap is completely deromanticized. Twain's Pap is a violent, heavy drinking, murderous, racist villain, and, unlike the makers of the anime or American film adaptations, Twain offers no description of Huck sorrowing over Pap's death. The anime also adds a subplot about the reunion of a mother and daughter that is not from Twain (*HFB,* episode 16). The anime's sentimental representation of family relationships might be a reflection of the expectations of its viewers. As mentioned, *Huckleberry Finn no Boken* was shown during the Sunday dinnertime and its main audience was juvenile viewers and their parents. As family entertainment, it could not without difficulty have depicted the hero's father as a murderous villain. Unlike literature, television animation places the story right before the eyes of its audience, and that audience is much larger and wider than an audience of

12. See *The Adventures of Huckleberry Finn* (MGM, 1939); *Adventures of Huckleberry Finn* (Great Amwell, 1985); and *The Adventures of Huck Finn* (Disney, 1993). In the latter, especially, Pap is presented as a monstrous figure.

readers. Television anime is therefore generally more conservative than literature. It was natural for television animes to put an emphasis on family love out of consideration for its viewers.

Huckleberry Finn no Boken also emphasizes educational and didactic elements. The proposal for the anime stressed its educational value. Explaining the aim of the project, the proposal called it a "serious and enjoyable anime based on world classic literature" that "contributes to the character formation of children who will shoulder the future of the new era."[13] The producers surely realized that Twain's Huck was too untamed for such a project. As was common among Japanese juvenile translations, therefore, Huck was again made considerably more genteel. He does not smoke or steal, but rather is a role model for child viewers. He works hard to return three dollars he has borrowed and courageously tells the King and Duke, "It is a bad thing to steal other people's property. It is bad" (*HFB,* episode 24). The series' ending clearly demonstrates its didacticism. In Twain's original, Huck, rejecting the idea of being "sivilized" again, says his famous words: "I reckon I got to light out for the Territory ahead of the rest" (*HF,* 366). In the anime, Huck is sent back to St. Petersburg to be educated by the Widow Douglas's sister, Miss Watson (who is still alive, though she dies in the original book). Huck decides to study, convinced by the respectable people who tell him, "You young people have to study hard and change this horrible world" and "You have to study in order to stop creating a poor slave like Jim again" (*HFB,* episode 26). In this way, the producers succeeded in transforming the untamable Huck into a somewhat civilized good boy and convincing parents to allow their children to watch the series. As a result, however, they considerably weakened the image of Huck Finn as an unfettered free spirit and destroyed Twain's satirical point that, in a slaveholding society, even educated people such as ministers and teachers contribute to justifying the cruel social institution of slavery.

Four years after the start of the *Huckleberry Finn no Boken* series, another television anime adaptation of Twain's work appeared. *Tom Sawyer no Boken* (The adventures of Tom Sawyer) was the most popu-

13. Sasaki, "Proposal and Summary," 3.

lar and largest-scale anime adaptation of Twain. Produced by Nippon Animation, it was broadcast Sunday evenings on the Fuji Television Network in forty-nine episodes from January 6 to December 28, 1980. At a total length of almost twenty-four hours, it is undoubtedly the longest visual adaptation of Twain's work in the world (figs. 5, 6).

The high quality of this anime's artwork is immediately evident. As is always the case with Nippon Animation's meisaku anime series, the art is detailed and faithful. Everything from houses, schools, and steamboats to furniture, cooking utensils, toys, and stationery is carefully re-created. This is the style associated with Hayao Miyazaki, who worked for Nippon Animation in the 1970s and went on to become the acknowledged master of anime. Miyazaki left the company a year before the premiere of *Tom Sawyer no Boken,* but its images are almost as detailed as those in the other series he worked on.[14] The accurate representations were the result of painstaking research, including a trip to Hannibal and St. Louis. Such visits usually involved four to five people and lasted about ten days. The director and animators visited museums and towns related to the original story, making sketches and taking photos to aid them in their work.[15]

Although its imagery is very faithful, the characters and story are somewhat tamed in *Tom Sawyer no Boken.* Toshihide Kunimatsu wrote: "Watching this *Tom Sawyer,* I got the impression that . . . this anime's characters, in particular characters of children, seem more cute and genteel than Twain's original. Aren't Tom, Huck, and Ben more soiled, wilder, bad boys in the original?"[16] Huck in this anime is certainly more respectable. He lives in a comfortable treehouse and does not sleep "on door-steps in fine weather and in empty hogsheads in wet" as Twain's Huck does (*TS,* 64). He seldom smokes and never uses racist language. As we have seen, bowdlerized characters are common in

14. Those series were *Arupusu no Shoujo Haiji* (Heidi, girl of the Alps; 1974), *Haha wo Tazunete Sanzenri* (Cuore: 7,500 miles looking for the mother, 1976), *Araiguma Rasukaru* (Rascal the raccoon; 1977), and *Akage no An* (Anne of Green Gables; 1979). Miyazaki left Nippon Animation before the completion of *Anne of Green Gables* to focus on directing his first animated feature film, *Rupan 3-sei Caliostro no Shiro* (Lupin III: The castle of Cagliostro; 1979). Matsumoto, *Twentieth-Century Television Readers,* 44–45.

15. Junzo Nakajima, interview by author, August 22, 2002, Tokyo.

16. Kunimatsu, "Waiting for a Dirtier Tom Sawyer," 46.

Figs. 5, 6. Tom Sawyer (*left*) and Huckleberry Finn (*right*) as they appeared in the 1980 animated adaptation of *The Adventures of Tom Sawyer.* Reprinted by permission of Nippon Animation Co., Ltd., from the covers of the video version of *Tom Sawyer no Boken,* vols. 1 and 2, 1980. © Nippon Animation Co., Ltd., 1980.

2
トム・ソーヤーの冒険
THE ADVENTURES OF TOM SAWYER

animations, and this anime's Huck follows that convention. In addition, just as Pap was humanized in the *Huckleberry Finn* anime, Injun Joe was humanized here. The anime's Joe is not a murderous villain who plans to take revenge on Widow Douglas by cutting her nose and ears. When Joe runs into Tom and Becky in the cave, he reassures them by saying that he wouldn't even think of killing children (*TSB,* episode 48). Instead of dying slowly of starvation in the cave, he falls to his death from a cliff. This anime, like the *Huckleberry Finn* anime, was dinnertime family entertainment, so it is natural that the elements of violence and cruelty embodied in Twain's Injun Joe were toned down in consideration of juvenile viewers.

More importantly, one of the most significant aspects of the original *Tom Sawyer,* the satirization of the townspeople's hypocrisy, is almost entirely missing from the anime. In Twain's original, for instance, there is a scene at a Sunday school where the townspeople start "showing off" to impress a prestigious visitor (*TS,* 48–49). Elsewhere, Twain satirizes the townspeople's changeable attitude toward the town drunkard, Muff Potter, who is suspected of murder. The same people who shouted for a lynching suddenly change their tune and acclaim Muff as a hero when he is proved to be innocent (*TS,* 189). The anime simply omits these scenes. As Akira Miyazaki, the scenario writer, put it, Twain's satirical story was turned into "a more casual adventure" for the anime adaptation.[17] It seems natural that Twain's satire and social criticism were avoided, since they would be too depressing for a supposedly cheerful family entertainment. Moreover, they would have clashed with the anime's nostalgic small-town images. Except for a few characters such as Pap Finn, Injun Joe, and Dobbins the schoolteacher, the local people are depicted as caring and good-hearted. In contrast to the *Huckleberry Finn* anime, there are no townspeople who despise Huck as an underclass homeless boy. As a result of this emphasis on the favorable aspects of the townspeople, Twain's satire of them was overlooked.[18]

17. Akira Miyazaki, interview by author, August 22, 2002, Tokyo. See also Kunimatsu, "Waiting for a Dirtier Tom Sawyer," 46–47.

18. Most American film adaptations of *Tom Sawyer* have also neglected Twain's satire of the townspeople in favor of a nostalgic emphasis on small-town America. Perry June Frank, "*The Adventures of Tom Sawyer* on Film: The Evolution of an American Icon," 131, 406.

However, the anime should not be compared with Twain's *Tom Sawyer* exclusively. Although *Tom Sawyer* was the main source, other influences are evident here and there. Akira Miyazaki recalled that it was not an easy task to write forty-nine episodes while sticking to only one book, so he borrowed some episodes from Twain's other works. For instance, in one scene in the anime, a riverboat pilot says to his apprentice: "Look at the surface. The surface of the river is the same as a book. You should learn how to read the book of the surface" (*TSB,* episode 8). In *Life on the Mississippi,* Twain uses the same metaphor to explain the art of piloting. "The Celebrated Jumping Frog of Calaveras Country" was the inspiration for another scene. Reflecting the conservative norms of television, however, there is no betting in this scene and the boy who cheats in the jumping-frog contest is punished in the end (*TSB,* episode 19). Even some of Twain's minor stories inspired Miyazaki, and as a result he wrote a long section based on *Tom Sawyer Abroad* in which Tom and Huck take a ride in a balloon (*TSB,* episodes 34–37).[19]

Undoubtedly, the outside source that had the greatest impact on the anime was *Adventures of Huckleberry Finn.* In fact, Miyazaki was more interested in *Huckleberry Finn* than he was in *Tom Sawyer.* He says, "I think *Huckleberry Finn* is a superior literary work mainly because it deals with more serious issues such as racism and slavery."[20] However, since a *Huckleberry Finn* anime had already appeared on television, Miyazaki found himself adapting *Tom Sawyer.* In his scenario, influences from *Huckleberry Finn* are everywhere. There are appearances by both Pap Finn and the slave Jim (not a black boy named Jim, as in the original *Tom Sawyer*) and, as in *Huckleberry Finn,* Huck and Tom both travel downriver and visit Tom's aunt in Arkansas.

As testimony to Akira Miyazaki's interest in racism and slavery, these themes are perhaps the most significant influence from *Huckleberry Finn.* Although Twain completely neglected the issue of slavery in *Tom Sawyer,* one episode of the anime focuses on the subject. In this episode, Tom and Jim help Morris, a runaway slave, to escape from slave hunters. Just as Huck in Japanese adaptations helps Jim without

19. Miyazaki, interview. For the riverboat pilot scene, see Mark Twain, *Life on the Mississippi,* 118–21.
20. Miyazaki, interview.

any second thoughts, Tom never hesitates to help Morris. Also like the Japanese version of Huck, Tom is unbelievably ignorant about the common rules of his slaveholding society. He is surprised to hear from Jim that to help a runaway slave is a "serious crime." Even then, he builds a raft for Morris's escape to Cairo, Illinois (*TSB*, episode 33). Although it is plausible that Huck, a social outsider, would help a runaway slave, it is unimaginable for Tom, a member of a respectable family, to be so willing to help. Miyazaki understands that Tom's actions in his scenario are unrealistic and might draw criticism from Americans, who are naturally more familiar with the history of slavery in their country than are the Japanese. At the same time, he feels his Tom is more understandable to a Japanese audience and especially to Japanese children, who are unfamiliar with American history.[21]

The ending of this episode seems to symbolize the difficulty in dealing with issues of race and slavery in a Japanese anime. After seeing Morris off on the raft, Tom naively asks Jim, "Do you also want to go to Cairo?" Jim responds with silence. Tom, realizing how thoughtless his question was, apologizes. This is the only scene in which Tom clearly recognizes Jim as a slave. Throughout, Jim is depicted as Aunt Polly's hardworking handyman and seems to be satisfied with his life. If the scenario had explored Jim's life as a slave more deeply, it would have ruined the harmonious atmosphere of a nostalgic story of small-town America. Tom and Jim avoid further talk about slavery, and there is no further exploration of the issue in the series. Although four episodes are devoted to Tom and Huck's trip down the river to Arkansas, they do not deal with issues of race and slavery but are mainly about a legendary wild white horse and people's attempts to catch it (*TSB*, episodes 42–45). Even so, despite Twain's neglect of the issue of slavery in *Tom Sawyer*, the tendency of television animes to avoid grave social issues, and Japanese viewers' lack of familiarity with the history of American slavery, the series at least pays attention to the issue of slavery in one episode. Considering all those difficulties, that should be counted as one of its achievements.

In addition, perhaps for the first time in Japanese juvenile versions of *Tom Sawyer*, the elements of romantic love in the original were re-

21. Ibid.

created and sometimes even emphasized. Not only did the scenario faithfully adapt Tom and Becky's famous engagement scene, which had been deleted in previous Japanese versions, but it also added new love stories.[22] For instance, Tom and Becky enjoy a romantic steamboat trip together, and even Huck falls in love, with a child actress named Lizet. Sharing similar backgrounds as orphans, Huck and Lizet are attracted to each other, but due to Lizet's traveling schedule they are separated in the end (*TSB,* episodes 28–31). The anime's emphasis on love between boys and girls mirrored the liberation of relationships in postwar Japan. As seen by the prewar and wartime maxim "Danjo Shichi-sai ni shite Seki wo Onaju sezu" (After the age of seven, males and females should not keep company with each other), Japanese boys and girls were strictly separated until the end of World War II. When the *Tom Sawyer no Boken* anime was produced, however, it had already been more than thirty years since coeducation in Japanese public schools was established by the Fundamental Law of Education in 1947. In contrast with prewar Japanese children, postwar boys and girls in Japan enjoyed more chances to interact with each other. In the early 1980s, even in elementary schools, precocious boys and girls exchanged love letters and diaries to show their affection. It also became common for girls to give Valentine chocolates to the boys they liked (though boys were not expected to give chocolates to girls). Times had changed, and there was no reason for an anime to avoid dealing with romance even when its main viewers were children.

In fact, Japanese animes are sometimes considered too liberated for American viewers and romantic elements are eliminated in the American versions. For instance, the *New York Times* reported that "the romance and girlish interplay that dominated" *Cardcaptor Sakura* (1998), a popular television anime in Japan, was "written out almost entirely" in Warner Brothers' version. The article said: "No Japanese viewer would lift an eyebrow at the fact that the fourth-grader Sakura is not only smitten with Yukito, a high school junior, but actually spends an episode on a 'date' with him. But American viewers would be appalled.

22. For the deletion of the love story between Tom and Becky, see, in addition to the discussion on pp. 16 and 72, Hitoshi Ishida, "Distorted Translations of *Tom Sawyer*"; Katsuura, *Translations Then and Now,* 225–35; Nakagaki, "How *Tom Sawyer*'s Humor Was Assimilated to Japan," 35–36.

[In America] where sexual molestation . . . is a genuine concern, no one wants to assume innocence in a cartoon subplot."[23] Similarly, the four episodes showing the romance between Huck and Lizet were entirely eliminated in the American video version of *Tom Sawyer no Boken.*

The *Tom Sawyer no Boken* anime was also more progressive than its source in its representation of females. It is true that the female characters in the anime are traditional; they are basically moralistic, sympathetic, weak, and passive. Like Twain's Becky, the anime's Becky helplessly cries when she gets lost in the cave (*TSB,* episode 47). But she is more outgoing than her counterpart in the original. She jumps into the water with Tom and Huck and enjoys catching catfish with them (*TSB,* episode 23). She is less reserved and more frank about her feelings, telling Tom "I love you" without much hesitation (*TSB,* episode 25). Although it would be unimaginable from the reserved Becky in Twain's original, the anime's Becky even kisses Tom spontaneously (*TSB,* episode 41). Moreover, the anime devotes four entire episodes to an independent female character, Lizet, who makes her own living with her acting talent and a strong sense of professionalism. Needless to say, there is no such independent female character in Twain's original.

These changes reflected the transformation of Japanese society in the late twentieth century. Although Japanese women in 1980 were not liberated as women in America, which experienced the women's liberation movement in the 1960s and '70s, they became more independent as a result of the democratization following World War II. According to a famous Japanese saying, "What became strong after the war are women and socks" (socks made of durable nylon became available at reasonable prices in postwar Japan). Although this saying is discriminatory in the way it places women and material goods on the same level, it accurately describes the significant changes in Japanese society. Under the American occupation, women obtained the right to vote and to attend public universities. The percentage of female university students increased from 2.5 percent in 1960 to 12.3 percent in 1980.[24] The women's liberation movement in America also had an impact on

23. J. D. Considine, "Making Anime a Little Safer for Americans," *New York Times,* January 20, 2002, sec. 2, 33.

24. Teruko Inoue and Yumiko Ehara, eds., *Josei no Data Book* (Data book on women), 143.

many young Japanese women, who organized a variety of demonstrations and women's groups in the 1970s. Groups such as Shinjuku Lib Center and Tokyo Umum rejected monogamy and formed women's communes. Other women's organizations had more specific purposes, such as the removal of the ban on contraceptive pills and colearning of science at public schools.[25] Even Japanese girls were no longer satisfied with the traditional passive roles. Although most female anime characters were greatly feminized, a variety of television anime series with active and independent heroines became tremendously popular in the 1960s and the '70s, such as *Mahotsukai Sally* (Sally the witch; 1966), *Attack No. 1* (1969), *Ace wo Nerae!* (Go for the ace; 1973), and *Candy Candy* (1976). It was in this environment that an independent girl such as Lizet was introduced and Becky transformed into a more active character in the *Tom Sawyer* anime, whose audience was not only boys but also girls. The progressive representation of female characters in the anime was also a result of its makers' views. Miyazaki, the scenario writer, has said he tends to employ "a lively woman with strong independent mind" in his stories.[26]

Tom Sawyer no Boken achieved amazing popularity in Japan. Its highest viewer rating was 19.6 percent, and it had a 15.5 percent average-audience rating for the year.[27] This means that approximately 10 to 18 million people followed the series. Although it was not a faithful adaptation and weakened Twain's satire, it introduced the world of Tom and Huck—with accurate and beautiful artwork, love stories that had long been neglected, and active female characters—to millions of Japanese. Many of these viewers, their interest stimulated, must have gone back to the original *Tom Sawyer* and Twain's other works. In this sense, the anime contributed to the awakening of an interest in Twain among late twentieth-century Japanese readers. *Tom Sawyer no Boken* remains the most accessible visual adaptation of Twain's works in Japan. After the television series ended, it was made available for sale or rental on

25. Sogo Joseishi Kenkyukai (Society for research on women's history), ed., *Nihon Josei no Rekishi, Shiso to Bunka: On'na to Otoko no Nozomashii Kankei wo Mezashite* (History of Japanese women, thoughts, and culture: For better relationships between women and men), 247–48.

26. Miyazaki, interview.

27. Junzo Nakajima, letter to author, August 29, 2002.

video, laser disc, and now DVD, where it continues to influence Japanese images of Twain in the twenty-first century.

Huckleberry Finn Monogatari (The tale of Huckleberry Finn), the latest anime version of Twain's work, is without doubt the most unconventional. Produced by Enoki Films, it aired on the satellite channel of NHK, the public television network, from August 26, 1994, to March 3, 1995. With twenty-six episodes each around twenty-five minutes long, its total running time was almost twelve hours, the same length as the 1976 *Huckleberry Finn no Boken* anime.

Although the format of this anime was similar to that of the television adaptations previously discussed, anime trends had changed considerably by the 1990s. While television animes were still very popular, meisaku anime, which was generally slow-paced, quiet, and with less action, was out of fashion. Viewer ratings of meisaku anime series had dropped to the single digits, and some episodes were canceled for baseball games and special programs.[28] The trend had changed to fast-paced, carnivalesque, comical animes such as Rumiko Takahashi's *Urusei Yatsura* (Those obnoxious aliens; 1981) and *Ranma ½* (1989) and, for juvenile viewers, fantastic, action-oriented, heroic stories such as *Dragon Ball* (1986), *Sailor Moon* (1992), and, of course, *Pokemon* (1997).

Reflecting these trends, Twain's *Huckleberry Finn* was completely transformed in this latest adaptation. *Huckleberry Finn Monogatari* is also fast-paced, carnivalesque, comical, fantastic, action-oriented, and heroic. It begins with a fight between Huck and a monster catfish. Huck hooks the fish on his line and is pulled deep into the water, only to be thrown high in the air by the force of the fish (*HFM*, episode 1). This opening scene sets the tone of the series. In a later episode, the story takes on the characteristics of a fairy tale. Huck, now famous as a

28. Matsumoto, *Twentieth-Century Television Readers,* 151. In 1997, Nippon Animation put an end to twenty-eight years of meisaku anime television series, partly because of juvenile audiences' unfamiliarity with classic literature. A spokesperson for Fuji Television Network explained: "Nowadays, many children haven't ever heard of the works of world classic literature. Since we thought it wouldn't be a good idea to show things that are not familiar, we decided to temporarily close this anime series." "Anime 'Sekai Meisaku Anime Gekijo' 28 nenkan no Hoso ni Owakare" (Anime "World Classic Theater" farewell to twenty-eight years of on-air history), *Asahi Shimbun,* March 10, 1997, evening ed., sec. 11.

hunter of catfish in the Mississippi, is asked to help a princess out of a dungeon by defeating another monster catfish. He succeeds with the help of a witch, a fairy, and a white unicorn (*HFM,* episode 16). Clearly, anything can happen in this anime, which, like other juvenile television animes in the 1980s and '90s, easily blends reality and fantasy.

The Huck in this anime incorporates Tom Sawyer's heroism, as described in Twain's *Tom Sawyer* and *Huckleberry Finn,* into his own character. Here, it is not Tom but Huck who goes to his own funeral and enjoys watching the townspeople's sorrow over his supposed death, and it is not Tom but Huck who helps Becky out of the cave (*HFM,* episodes 10, 4). Huck's heroic deeds can also be very comical. For instance, he knows that Injun Joe has a weak point, which is fear of mice. During his fight against Joe, Huck lets hundreds of mice out of a bag and scares Joe into running away (*HFM,* episode 4). Although the situations were different, similar kinds of comical fighting were common in television anime in the 1980s and '90s. For instance, the boy hero of *Urusei Yatsura* achieves victory over a female alien by stealing the top of her bikini.[29] Huck's comical heroism in *Huckleberry Finn Monogatari* was undoubtedly influenced by such animes. In all of his heroic deeds, Huck acts energetically and courageously. There is no shadow of the indecisiveness that Twain's Huck frequently but realistically shows. The original Huck's complexity is almost totally neglected. This anime turns Huck into the kind of clear-cut hero that matched the taste of juvenile viewers who favored heroic and fantastic shows such as *Kin'niku Man* (Muscle man), *Dragon Ball,* and *Pokemon.*

Having chosen to emphasize action and heroic adventures, the producers avoided the controversial issues presented in their source. Instead, they borrowed episodes and characters from *Tom Sawyer,* which is less controversial. In addition to Becky and Injun Joe, such well-known episodes as the treasure hunt and the exploration of the cave are employed (*HFM,* episodes 5–6). Following the genteel tradition of Japanese juvenile translations and adaptations of *Huckleberry Finn,* the anime also considerably tames its main character. Images of smoking and drinking are absent, since they were prohibited by the broadcasting

29. "Uwasa no Rum-chan Dacchu!" episode 1 of *Urusei Yatsura,* dir. Mamoru Oshii, Kitty Film Fuji, Fuji Television Network, October 14, 1981.

code for juvenile television anime.[30] Also, although the series is full of action, there is no real violence, despite the fact that events such as murder and lynching are common in the original. The bloody fighting in the feud between the Grangerfords and the Shepherdsons is turned into an exchange of abusive words and the throwing of tomatoes (*HFM,* episodes 17–18), and Pap Finn is not even murdered. Evil characters such as Injun Joe and the King and Duke are turned into comical characters. As in the 1976 anime of *Huckleberry Finn,* Pap Finn is not as despicable as he is in the original. He is still a drunkard and tries to steal Huck's money, but he is also kind enough to cover Huck with a blanket as he sleeps and to prepare a big meal to make Huck happy (*HFM,* episode 9). Even though almost twenty years had passed since the first *Huckleberry Finn* anime, it was still difficult for a family series to depict a father as an absolute villain. As a result of this anime's avoidance of elements of violence and evil, it almost completely misses Twain's satire and turns *Huckleberry Finn* into a somewhat optimistic and sentimental adventure story.

The most surprising alteration is that of Jim, who is changed from a runaway slave, husband, and father to a free black boy. Unrealistically for a black boy in the nineteenth-century American South, he mixes with whites without any difficulty and is unconcerned with issues of racial identity. Although he and Huck travel down the Mississippi on a raft, the journey is not undertaken to gain his freedom. Instead, it is a sentimental journey to see his mother, who is ill. As a result of the elimination of the original Jim, issues of slavery and race are entirely ignored in this anime. One can tell that it is situated in nineteenth-century America from the frequent appearances of steamboats and other period commodities, but it is hard to tell that it is set in the slaveholding antebellum South. The 1976 *Huckleberry Finn* anime focused on the relationship between Huck and Jim by eliminating Tom from the story, which enabled it to pay more attention to issues of race and slavery. The 1994 anime, by eliminating the original Jim, turned Twain's novel into a deracialized adventure story. Although the title of the anime is *The Tale of Huckleberry Finn,* it is not the story of Twain's Huck.

30. Enoki, interview.

The utter absence of issues of race and slavery resulted partly from a concern about the representation of blacks. Since the anime was produced not only for the Japanese public but also for the global market, it was necessary for the producers to follow global standards—in particular, American culturally sensitive norms about the representation of blacks. It is difficult in the American juvenile television anime market to represent black characters in extreme poverty or with very dark complexions.[31] Following these conventions, the anime portrayed the boy Jim in respectable clothing and with a light complexion (fig. 7). In Japan as well, awareness and sensitivity toward the representation of blacks had started to increase. In 1988 the *Washington Post* and African American political organizations criticized Japanese translations of Helen Bannerman's *The Story of Little Black Sambo* (1899) and the manufacture of caricaturized black dolls in Japan.[32] The initial *Post* article drew thousands of letters of protest addressed to the Japanese embassy and caused African American congressmen to organize a boycott of Japanese products. In response to those criticisms, the books and dolls were quickly removed from Japanese stores. Stimulated by the American criticism, books and essays criticizing Japanese racism against blacks were published in Japan from the late 1980s to the early '90s and many of the stereotype dolls and books were prohibited.[33] Japanese manga and anime were notorious for their caricaturized representations of blacks. In the 1960s, executives at the NBC television network asked Osamu Tezuka to modify the black characters in his *Jungle Taitei* (Jungle emperor) anime. He rejected their suggestions and kept creating highly stereotyped images of blacks.[34] However, works with racial caricature were no longer viable in the era of globalization in the 1990s. It is possible that the producers of the 1994 *Huckleberry Finn* anime overreacted to the recent attacks on Japanese

31. Ibid.

32. See Margaret Shapiro, "Old Black Stereotypes Find New Lives in Japan: Marketers Defend Sambo Toys, Black Mannequins, Insist Racism Was Not Intended," *Washington Post,* July 22, 1988, sec. A, 18; Margaret Shapiro, "Japanese Companies Recall 'Little Black Sambo' Products," *Washington Post,* July 29, 1988, sec. A, 15.

33. John G. Russell, "Consuming Passions: Spectacle, Self-Transformation, and the Commodification of Blackness in Japan."

34. Russell, *Japanese Images of Blacks,* 86–89.

Fig. 7. Huck and Jim on the raft in the 1994 animated adaptation of *Huckleberry Finn.* Reproduced by permission of Enoki Films Co., Ltd., from *Huckleberry Finn Monogatari.* © Enoki Films Co., Ltd., 1994.

representations of blacks and eliminated all elements of race, along with Twain's Jim, in order to avoid any criticism.

What is most progressive about *Huckleberry Finn Monogatari* is its representation of female characters. While the 1980 *Tom Sawyer* anime made progress in this area, the 1994 anime was more liberal in its representation of women. For instance, Becky in 1994 is more active than Becky in 1980. With Tom and Huck, she even enjoys catching frogs, which are usually regarded as one of the most detested animals among Japanese women (*HFM,* episode 2). She also courageously protests against the townspeople who suspect Huck to be a thief (*HFM,* episode 2). Miss Watson, a conservative, middle-aged lady in Twain's original, is transformed into an uninhibited young woman who enjoys flying a kite and climbing a tree (figs. 8, 9). Even a minor character such as Judith Loftus, who in the original shrewdly sees through Huck's disguise when he is dressed as a girl, is made to be more aggressive. In the anime, she is an expert shot and saves Huck and Jim by heroically chasing off some dangerous villains (*HFM,* episode 11).

Although Japan in the twenty-first century is still a male-dominated society in many ways, it is also true that, like American women, Japanese women became more empowered in the period from the late 1970s to the early '90s. For instance, the Equal Employment Opportunity Law for Men and Women was passed in 1986 to encourage women to enter the workplace, and more women started holding administrators' positions in Japanese companies in the early 1990s. In 1992, only 38.2 percent of Japanese companies had at least one female administrator, but that number jumped to 72.1 percent in 1995.[35] Although it lasted only a few years, the so-called "Madonna Boom" in the 1988 election caused a dramatic increase in women in the Diet, providing women with more political power. Anime in the 1980s and early '90s also pushed against conventional stereotypes of female characters. For example, while the heroine of *Sailor Moon* is very sexualized in appearance, she is an empowered character with magical abilities. In addition, female heroines who break the conventional stereotype are common in the works of Hayao Miyazaki, the leading

35. Economic Planning Agency, "Hataraku Josei: Atarashii Shakai Shisutemu wo Motomete" (Working women: For a new social system), 1.

Fig. 8. An illustration of Miss Watson from the original American edition of *Huckleberry Finn.* Samuel L. Clemens, *Adventures of Huckleberry Finn* (New York: Charles L. Webster and Company, 1885), 19.

Fig. 9. Miss Watson in the 1994 animated adaptation of *Huckleberry Finn*. Reproduced by permission of Enoki Films Co., Ltd., from *Huckleberry Finn Monogatari*. © Enoki Films Co., Ltd., 1994.

figure in Japanese anime in the 1980s and '90s. Susan J. Napier writes, "Unlike the classic *shojo* [little girl], who is usually characterized by an ultra femininity that is often passive or dreamy . . . , Miyazaki's girl characters are notably independent and active, courageously confronting the variety of obstacles before them in a manner that might well be described as stereotypically masculine."[36] The liberated and empowered female characters in the 1994 *Huckleberry Finn* anime obviously mirrored these contemporary trends. It was meant to appeal to young female viewers who preferred to see liberated and empowered female characters in their animes.

While, as we have seen, this anime utterly neglected the serious issues and historical realism in Twain's *Huckleberry Finn,* it would not be fair to criticize it without considering the fact that it was produced in a truly difficult time and situation. The genre of meisaku anime was already out of fashion in Japanese television when the series was produced. The budget for production became tighter. As a result, the production company could no longer afford to pay for detailed background research, such as intensive research trips, as in the 1970s and '80s, the golden age of meisaku anime.[37] However, the series still had to survive in the Japanese anime market, which is undoubtedly the most competitive anime market in the world. Considering these difficulties, it is understandable that the producers avoided dealing with serious and complicated issues. But even with all their assimilation to contemporary trends, their anime did not have a chance to be aired on a regular television channel. It aired instead on the satellite channel of public television, which traditionally had strong educational tendencies. In short, this anime could survive only under the protection of an educational institution and public capital. The prestige of *Huckleberry Finn* as a classic of world literature must have greatly contributed to providing the opportunity to air the anime on educational public television.

Public television is still willing to air meisaku anime series, but the meisaku anime boom has long been over and it is unlikely that current regular television channels in Japan will air meisaku anime. However, in the sphere of theatrical feature anime, the meisaku anime tradition

36. Napier, *Anime from* Akira *to* Princess Mononoke, 124.
37. Enoki, interview.

is still alive. The tradition continues in the works of Hayao Miyazaki and Isao Takahata, who also worked at Nippon Animation in the 1970s and later formed Studio Ghibli with Miyazaki. Some of their animes are adaptations of literary works, and they have been both artistically and commercially successful. For example, Miyazaki's *Majo no Takkyubin* (Kiki's delivery service; 1989) is an adaptation of juvenile novelist Eiko Kadono's book of the same name. Takahata's acclaimed *Hotaru no Haka* (Grave of the fireflies; 1988) is a faithful adaptation of a short story by postwar novelist Akiyuki Nosaka. Someday, perhaps, talented anime artists such as Miyazaki and Takahata will creatively and faithfully adapt Twain's works as theatrical features and introduce them to a wider Japanese public in the twenty-first century.

The television anime adaptations discussed above transformed Twain's *Huckleberry Finn* and *Tom Sawyer* in a number of ways. Following the unwritten code of television anime for family entertainment, they all altered the originals to create certain kinds of characters, such as clear-cut heroes, a humanized father, and a genteel Huck Finn. Each anime also reflected the trends of a particular era in Japanese anime and society at large, such as awareness of the American civil rights movement in the 1960s, the boom of television meisaku anime series in the 1970s and '80s, oversensitivity toward the representation of blacks in the late 1980s, the faster pace of juvenile television anime in the 1980s and '90s, and the empowerment of women toward the close of the century. In this way, Tom Sawyer and Huck Finn, two of the most significant American fictional icons, were transformed to fit into late twentieth-century Japanese culture.

At the same time, however, similar transformations were evident in American adaptations of *Tom Sawyer* and *Huckleberry Finn,* especially Hollywood adaptations. Therefore, we cannot say that such changes are distinctively Japanese. Twain's works challenge conservative cultural norms not only in Japan but also in America. American film adaptations of *Tom Sawyer* and *Huckleberry Finn* also avoid racist terms, violence, and other controversial representations as a result of their consideration for juvenile viewers. As early as the 1930s, the Hayes Office censored a *Tom Sawyer* film, deleting scenes in which Huck shared his pipe with other boys. The characters of Huck and Tom have been made more genteel in Hollywood as well as Japanese adaptations.[38] For instance, Elijah Wood in Disney's *The Adventures of Huck Finn* (1993) seems too young and cute for the role of Huck. In this, the movie followed the example of Norman Rockwell's well-known illustrations of Huck and Tom. Perry June Frank writes, "Rockwell's illustrations characterize the boys as smaller and younger than Twain's descriptions would suggest, and Huck and Tom have an all-American 'cuteness' that conflicts with the serious elements in the novels."[39] Moreover, the Disney *Huck Finn,* like the 1976 Japanese anime, eliminated Tom Sawyer from the story and focused on the relationship between Huck and Jim. Finally, just as in the 1980 *Tom Sawyer* anime, idealized nostalgic images of American small-town life were emphasized in Hollywood's *Tom Sawyer* films, and, as a result, Twain's satire of the townspeople was also neglected in those films.

The fact that many of the changes in the Japanese anime adaptations were not "distinctively Japanese" demonstrates that certain cultural tendencies in America are shared with other countries and cause similar transformations of culture. As we have seen, America and Japan both experienced the empowerment of women and challenges to stereotypical portrayals of blacks in the late twentieth century (although on a much smaller scale in Japan), resulting in similar transformations of cultural texts, such as visual adaptations of Twain's works, in both countries. In this way, the Japanese anime adaptations of Twain demonstrate that most culture is globally shared and that a country's "cultural uniqueness" can be hard to find given the impact of cultural globalization in the late twentieth century.

However, although many of the alterations made in the Japanese Twain animes also appear in the American adaptations, some of them would be unimaginable in America. First, though American adaptations of *Huckleberry Finn* can be superficial, none eliminates Jim and ignores issues of race and slavery as the 1994 Japanese anime does.[40]

38. The two 1930s films were *The Adventures of Tom Sawyer,* dir. Norman Taurog, United Artists, 1938, and *The Adventures of Huckleberry Finn,* dir. Richard Thorpe, MGM, 1939. See Frank, "*The Adventures of Tom Sawyer* on Film," 89, 258; Perry June Frank, "*Adventures of Huckleberry Finn* on Film."

39. Frank, "*The Adventures of Tom Sawyer* on Film," 76.

40. A possible exception is the American stage adaptation of Twain that Shelley Fisher Fishkin described as follows: "No Jim. No black actors in the entire cast. And

The neglect of race issues in the Japanese anime seems to demonstrate unfamiliarity or indifference concerning race issues in Japan, which is of course a racially homogeneous country compared to racially diversified America. Second, no characters appear naked in the American film adaptations. In contrast, in the 1980 *Tom Sawyer* anime, Tom and Huck frequently appear stark naked and are drawn anatomically correct (*TSB*, episodes 1, 14). This is partly due to the difference between broadcasting codes in Japan and America.[41] It also reflects the difference between the two countries' perceptions of nudity, particularly child nudity. Compared to America, Japan is traditionally liberal about nudity. Although mixed bathing became rare in the twentieth century, it is still common for parents to take baths with their preteen children. Most Japanese viewers just did not care about the nudity of Tom and Huck. Of course, those scenes were eliminated in the American versions of the anime. There are six American video versions of the 1980 *Tom Sawyer* anime, and none of them show Huck and Tom naked. Finally, the American film adaptations transform the sources to a lesser degree than do the Japanese animes. No American adaptation includes such radical transformations as Huck battling a monster catfish or the replacement of the runaway slave Jim by a free black boy. Although one would not call them excellent, the American film adaptations generally show more respect for Twain's originals.[42] The differences between the degree of faithfulness in the Japanese and American

---

no reference to the fact that both Hannibal and the fictionalized version of it in Twain's novels had been a slaveholding town." This was not a popular adaptation of *Huckleberry Finn,* however, but a local production presented at Huck's Homestead Restaurant in Hannibal, Missouri, and based on "[e]pisodes from *Tom Sawyer, Huckleberry Finn,* and *Life on the Mississippi.*" Fishkin, *Lighting Out for the Territory,* 39–40.

41. Nakajima, interview.

42. Perhaps the most faithful American adaptation is *Adventures of Huckleberry Finn,* dir. Peter H. Hunt, Great Amwell Company/PBS, 1985. Although this television film considerably shortened the controversial ending of the book, it faithfully re-created, in four hour-long episodes, most of the dark episodes in the novel. In his study of American film adaptations of *Huckleberry Finn,* Clyde V. Haupt calls this film "simply the best, most demanding Huck adaptation made to date. Set apart from all other Huck films, it effectively and faithfully parallels its source novel to an uncommon degree; few film adaptations of any novel are this accurate to their source text." Clyde V. Haupt, *Huckleberry Finn on Film: Film and Television Adaptations of Mark Twain's Novel, 1920–1993,* 176.

adaptations reflect different public perceptions of Twain's works. The Japanese respect *Huckleberry Finn* as a world classic, but they do not admire it as they do representative works of Japanese literature. The Japanese public is also not as familiar with Twain and the historical background of his works. In America, Mark Twain is a national icon and *Huckleberry Finn* a cornerstone of the national literature.[43] In America, criticisms of shallow adaptations of Twain's works are more severe. Considering the level of respect for Twain among Americans, it seems reasonable that American film adaptations would be more faithful to the originals than Japanese anime adaptations.

Although the Japanese animes are basically unfaithful to Twain's originals, they are very faithful to juvenile anime viewers' expectations in the late twentieth century. All three of the animes discussed above were welcomed in the global market. Although the 1976 *Huckleberry Finn* anime seems not to have aired on television networks outside of Japan, the series was edited in 1984 into a 72-minute English version, called *The Raft Adventures of Huck and Jim,* for sale in the American video market. It is still available today and is the most popular animated version of *Huckleberry Finn* in America. The global popularity of Nippon Animation's 1980 *Tom Sawyer* anime was tremendous. It was shown on major television networks in most of the countries in Europe and Southeast Asia. (Chinese television did not broadcast it since authorities did not want children exposed to a hero who "plays hooky"). Even in America, where the strength of domestic popular culture tends to inhibit the acceptance of other countries' cultural products, HBO purchased the right to show the anime at a European anime festival and air it in America on its cable television network in 1988—"the first Japanese animated program acquired and telecast by the channel," according to Nippon Animation.[44] This anime was adapted and marketed in various video versions in America under the title *The All New Adventures of Tom Sawyer* (Celebrity Home Entertainment, 1991, 1992, 1995). The Japanese original had to be considerably bowdlerized to fit into the puritanical tradition of American juvenile ani-

43. See Louis J. Budd, "Mark Twain as an American Icon."
44. Nakajima, interview; Nippon Animation home page, http://www.nipponanimation.com/history/main.html.

mation, and scenes with nudity, tobacco, and drinking were censored.[45] The various versions of this anime are still the most commonly available *Tom Sawyer* animations in America. As for the 1994 *Huckleberry Finn* anime, it was produced with international partners from the start; an Italian television network shared the cost of production with Enoki Films. This anime was translated into most major languages and aired in approximately 110 countries.[46]

The global acceptance of the Japanese *Tom Sawyer* and *Huckleberry Finn* animes is just one example of the global popularity and acceptance of Japanese anime in the late twentieth century. As far back as the 1960s, Japanese animes such as *Astro Boy, Gigantor,* and *Speed Racer* enjoyed great popularity among television viewers in America. In 1982 the Japanese theatrical feature anime *Macross* was released in an Americanized version called *Robotech.* The global popularity and impact of Japanese anime in the 1990s is truly amazing. In 1992, Japan exported 4.8 times as many animes as in 1980. In 1996, Disney signed a deal to release video and theatrical versions of Hayao Miyazaki's animes in America. That same year, Hollywood director James Cameron asked anime director Oshii Mamoru to cooperate on a new film project, but they failed to reach an agreement. Soon afterward, *Pokemon* swept America, becoming a social phenomenon and *Time* magazine cover story in 1999.[47] The international celebration of Japanese animes have encouraged the global acceptance of the *Huckleberry Finn* and *Tom Sawyer* series.

Anime, as a visual art form, is suitable for transcending borders. As many viewers have remarked, most Japanese anime characters do not look Japanese; with their bigger eyes, lighter complexions, and higher nose bridges, they look more like westerners. While this certainly shows the Japanese obsession with Western appearance, it also demonstrates

45. Nakajima, interview.
46. Enoki, interview.
47. "The History of Animania," *Time,* December 22, 1999, 96; Yuka Kuwahata, "Nihon Anime ni Sekai ga Nesshisen" (Global fascination with Japanese anime), *Aera,* July 29, 1996, 8; Andrew Pollack, "Disney in Pact for Films of the Top Animator in Japan," *New York Times,* July 24, 1996, sec. D, 1; Howard Chua-Eoan and Tim Larimer, "Pokemania: Can Such Cute Critters Be Bad Influences? How One Misfit's Quest Turned into a Global Bonanza," *Time,* September 22, 1999, 80–93.

that anime can easily transcend limitations of race and nationality.[48] It is also much easier than in live-action films to employ international settings, since filmmakers do not need to actually go to locations outside Japan and hire foreign actors. There is no doubt that the transnational characteristics of anime were advantageous for the *Tom Sawyer* and *Huckleberry Finn* series when they were exported for international viewers. Although they are in fact Japanese, global viewers can easily forget their origins and enjoy them as American stories.

The Japanese anime versions of *Tom Sawyer* and *Huckleberry Finn* clearly demonstrated that the globalization of culture does not flow only in one direction. As we have seen, Twain was first introduced by America to Japan in the 1890s. By the 1970s, more than one hundred translations of his works had been published in Japan. After all those efforts to assimilate Twain's works into their own culture, the Japanese finally created versions of Twain's works, the *Tom Sawyer* and *Huckleberry Finn* animes, that were introduced by Japan to America. These animes were seen by millions of Americans and must have influenced their perceptions of *Tom Sawyer* and *Huckleberry Finn.* After almost eighty years of one-way assimilation of Twain's works, there was now a two-way interaction. In this sense, the Japanese anime versions of *Tom Sawyer* and *Huckleberry Finn* marked an epoch in the history of Mark Twain in Japan.

48. For the "statelessness" of Japanese animes, see Napier, *Anime from* Akira *to* Princess Mononoke, 24–27.

Conclusion

As demonstrated in this book, Japan has transformed Twain's works in various ways since its first encounter with him a hundred years ago, and those versions of his works were shared by millions of Japanese. While this is the first book-length study of Twain's impact on Japanese popular culture and juvenile literature, it is not the last word on the subject. Japanese versions of Twain and his works are too diverse for a single project to cover. Twain is everywhere in Japan. On stage, for instance, *Tom Sawyer* was adapted as a musical in 1987. *Big River,* the award-winning Broadway musical adaptation of *Huckleberry Finn,* was performed in Tokyo and Osaka by a mostly Japanese cast in 1988 and was revived in Tokyo in 2004 (fig. 10). The musical group Takarazuka-kagekidan (Takarazuka operetta troupe) staged an adaptation of *A Connecticut Yankee in King Arthur's Court* in 1994. In the sphere of popular music, a rock group called Huckleberry Finn recently made its debut.[1] Japanese businesses do not ignore the market value of Mark

1. *Adventure Musical Tom Sawyer,* dir. Masaaki Osumi, July–August 1987; *Big River,* dir. Michael Greif, Aoyama Theater, Tokyo, March 4–May 5, 1988, Kintetsu

Fig. 10. Advertisement for the 2004 Tokyo revival of *Big River.* This revival, a production of the Deaf West Theater, was performed by deaf, hard-of-hearing, and hearing actors. Reprinted by permission of Horipro Inc.

Twain and his works. Nissin Foods used Tom Sawyer in its 1987 advertising campaign for Cup Noodle, calling him "the character that symbolizes Nissin Foods' pioneering spirit of enterprise." A 1992 television commercial for Misawa Home, a building company, featured Twain's house in Hartford, Connecticut, and his famous words: "My books are water; those of the great geniuses are wine. Everybody drinks water." In 1975, Twain himself appeared in a best-selling ninja novel set in the nineteenth century. The hero of the novel travels to Virginia City, Nevada, where he meets Twain, who is working as a newspaper man and who helps the hero solve the secret of a treasure hunt.[2] There is even a small theme park in Yonago City, Tottori, named Daisen Tom Sawyer Bokujo (Tom Sawyer ranch). However, none of its attractions are closely related to Twain's famous novel.

These Japanese versions of Twain and his works show that the recipients of culture are not always merely passive. Japan often asserted its autonomy by transforming, distorting, and even rejecting aspects of Twain and his works. Of course, in the process, significant elements of the originals were sometimes lost. As we have seen, the Japanese repeatedly neglected Twain's social satire and often cast him as a harmless

---

Theater, Osaka, May 10–29, 1988; *Big River,* dir. Jeff Calhoun, Aoyama Theater, Tokyo, September 28–October 24, 2004; *Aro Aro Camelot?* dir. Tetsunori Ota, Takarazuka Bau Hall, Osaka, May 29–June 12, 1994; *River Dance,* Huckleberry Finn, Kings Record, 2002. For reviews of the original Japanese production of *Big River,* see "The Play Was Deepened by the Black Actor" (note 12); "Kakkiteki na Hohoron no mae dewa, Dareshimo Kofuku na Kibun ni Nareru: *Big River* wo Megutte" (Everybody feels happy with an innovative methodology: A thought on *Big River*), *Tarzan,* May 25, 1988, 116–17. For an interview with the director, see "Musical Big River: Enshutsuka Michael Greif-shi ni Kiku" (Musical *Big River*: Interview with the director, Michael Greif), *Asahi Shimbun,* February 12, 1988, sec. 9, evening ed.

2. Nissin Shokuhin Kabushikigaisha Shashi Hensanshitsu, ed., *Shokutarite Yo wa Tairaka* (The history of Nissin Foods), 314; Nissin Shokuhin television commercial for Cup Noodle, 1987; Nissin Shokuhin newspaper advertisement for Cup Noodle, *Asahi Shimbun,* January 5, 1987; Misawa Home television commercial, dir. Sakutaro Nakagawa, 1992; Sakutato Nakagawa, interview by author, August 21, 2002, Tokyo; Tetsu Yano, *Kamui no Ken* (The sword of Kamui). A 1998 novel by Munenori Harada called *Heisei Tom Sawyer* is about high school students in Tokyo and barely mentions Twain's character. (*Heisei* is the name of the current imperial era, which started in 1989.)

children's novelist. Japan still needs more time to develop a deeper understanding of Twain.

However, I am not pessimistic about Twain's future in Japan. There are a variety of farsighted projects and serious scholarly efforts that aim to develop Japanese people's understanding of the complexity of Twain's works. Numerous articles are published every year, and Twain scholarship is thriving. Shelley Fisher Fishkin, writing about her experience as keynote speaker at the Kyoto American Studies Summer Seminar in 1999, noted the importance of international researchers to the field of American Studies and referred to the variety of efforts by Japanese Twain scholars. According to Fishkin, "Mark Twain studies in Japan are not just alive and well: as Twain himself would have said, they're 'booming.'"[3] The July 1996 issue of the Japanese literary magazine *Eureka* was devoted to Twain, and leading Japanese Twainians published insightful essays from a variety of perspectives. In 1997, the Japan Mark Twain Society was founded in response to enthusiastic requests by Japanese Twain scholars. The Society holds an annual academic conference, providing an opportunity for Japanese Twain scholars to exchange their thoughts and ideas. In 2002, the Society began publishing a superbly edited annual, the *Journal of Mark Twain Studies.* The first issue featured essays on the theme "Mark Twain and Technology" (fig. 11).[4] The Society launched an English-language journal in 2004. In addition, a number of faithful Japanese translations of Twain's writings have appeared recently. Japanese translators and scholars have revisited the difficult task of translating *Huckleberry Finn,* and we now have several fascinating translations of the novel in colloquial Japanese. Even Twain's love letters were carefully translated by Japanese Twainians recently.[5] The ambitious translation project of the

3. Shelley Fisher Fishkin, "Mark Twain in Japan," 5.

4. *Eureka: Shi to Hihyo* (Eureka: Poetry and criticism) 28:8 (July 1996), special issue on Mark Twain; Nihon Mark Twain Kyokai, ed., *Mark Twain: Kenkyu to Hihyo* (Journal of Mark Twain studies).

5. Keiko Nakagawa and Mitsuko Miyamoto, trans., *Mark Twain no Love Letter,* is a 1999 translation of *The Love Letters of Mark Twain,* ed. Dixon Wecter (New York: Harper, 1949). Recent translations of *Adventures of Huckleberry Finn,* all titled *Huckleberry Finn no Boken,* include those made by Takashi Nozaki (1971); Minoru Nishida (1977); Toshio Watanabe (1980); Choichi Yamamoto (1996); Yoshio Katsuura (1998); Hiroshi Okubo (1999); and Shozo Kajima (2001).

Fig. 11. The first issue of the *Journal of Mark Twain Studies,* April 2002. Reprinted by permission of Nan'undo Publishing Company.

recent Oxford edition of Twain's works has just been completed. There are twenty volumes in total and many of them are the first Japanese translations.[6] I believe that creative adaptations of Twain, stimulated by these efforts, will continue to appear in twenty-first-century Japan.

6. *The Oxford Mark Twain,* 29 vols., series ed. Shelley Fisher Fishkin (New York: Oxford University Press, 1996). Sairyusha Publishing Company's Mark Twain Collection, series ed. Kazuya Shigeyama, comprises translations of the following works: *Pudd'nhead Wilson and Those Extraordinary Twins; Life on the Mississippi; Letters from the Earth; No. 44, The Mysterious Stranger; The Adventures of Tom Sawyer; Adventures of Huckleberry Finn; A Tramp Abroad; 3,000 Years among the Microbes; The Innocents Abroad; Roughing It; The American Claimant; The Prince and the Pauper; Following the Equator; Letters from Hawaii; A Connecticut Yankee in King Arthur's Court; Mark Twain's Speeches; Europe and Elsewhere; The Gilded Age; What Is Man?* The twentieth volume in the series is Yoko Arima's study *Mark Twain Shin-kenkyu: Yume to Ban'nen no Fantasy* (A new perspective on Mark Twain: Dream and fantasy in his last years).

Appendix

Mark Twain and His Works in Japanese Twentieth-Century Popular Culture

Selected Sources

Translations and Adaptations

Twain's works and their translations are listed in order of publication date. Translations published after 1950 are too numerous to be included in full. This list therefore contains only a representative sampling of post-1950 translations, mainly those for adult readers.

"The Celebrated Jumping Frog of Calaveras County" (1867)

Sasaki, Kuni, trans. "Kake Kawazu." *Bungei Kurabu* 18:8 (1912): 67–77.

Souma, Taizo [Shozo Chiba], adapt. "Kakebaka no Sankichi." *Dowa* 6:5 (1925): 92–98.

Kagatani, Rinnosuke, trans. "Hanegaeru." In *Sekai wo Warawaseta Hiniku na Hanashi.* Tokyo: Shoryudo, 1926.

Yanagida, Izumi, trans. "Meibutsu Tobigaeru." In *Sekai Tanpen Shosetsu Taikei, America hen.* Tokyo: Kindaisha, 1926.

Sasaki, Kuni, trans. "Hane Gaeru." In *Mark Twain Meisaku Shu.* Tokyo: Kaizosha, 1929.

Ueno, Naozo, trans. "Calaveras-gun no Nadakaki Tobigaeru." In *Calaveras-gun no Nadakaki Tobigaeru, Kaibutsu.* Tokyo: Nan'undo, 1960.

Furusawa, Yasujiro, trans. "Uwasa ni Natta Calaveras Gun no Tobigaeru." In *Mark Twain Tanpenshu.* Tokyo: Shinchosha, 1961.

Nozaki, Takashi, trans. "Sonona mo Takaki Calaveras Gun no Tobigaeru." In *Sekai Tanpen Bungaku Zenshu, America Bungaku 19-seiki.* Tokyo: Shueisha, 1964.

Inoue, Kazuo, trans. "Sononamo Takaki Jump Gaeru." In *America Horabanashi.* Tokyo: Chikuma Shobo, 1968.

Sakashita, Noboru, "Sonona mo Takaki Calaveras Gun no Tobigaeru." In *Buck Fanshaw no Soshiki Hoka 13-pen.* Tokyo: Iwanami Shoten, 1977.

Okubo, Hiroshi, trans. "Jim Smiley to Kare no Daijina Tobigaeru." In *Shinsen Mark Twain Kessakushu.* Tokyo: Obunsha, 1985.

The Innocents Abroad (1869)

Hamada, Seijiro, trans. *Akagetto Gaiyuki.* 3 vols. Tokyo: Shingetsusha, 1949.

———. *Akagetto Gaiyuki.* 3 vols. Tokyo: Iwanami Shoten, 1951.

Yoshioka, Eiichi, Hiroyuki Nishikiori, and Eiichi Iizuka, trans., *Chichukai Yuranki.* 2 vols. Tokyo: Sairyusha, 1997.

Katsuura, Yoshio, and Katsuura Sumi, trans. *Innocent Abroad: Seichi Hatsu-junrei no Tabi.* 2 vols. Tokyo: Bunkashobo Hakubunsha, 2004.

Roughing It (1872)

Jingu, Teruo, trans. *Seibu Boken Ryoko.* In *Mark Twain Meisaku Zenshu,* vol. 6. Tokyo: Iwasaki Shoten, 1962.

Nozaki, Takashi, and Taro Komatsu, trans. *Seibu Ryoko Kidan.* Tokyo: Chikuma Shobo, 1969.

Yoshida, Eiko, and Toru Kiuchi, trans. *Seibu Horoki.* 2 vols. Tokyo: Sairyusha, 1998.

The Gilded Age (with Charles Dudley Warner, 1874)

Nasu, Yorimasa, trans. *Kinmekki Jidai.* 2 vols. Kyoto: Yamaguchi Shoten, 1980, 1982.

Kakinuma, Takako, and Hiroyuki Nishikiori, trans. *Kinmekki Jidai.* 2 vols. Tokyo: Sairyusha, 2001–2002.

The Adventures of Tom Sawyer (1876)

Sasaki, Kuni, trans. *Tom Sawyer Monogatari.* Tokyo: Katei Yomimono Kankokai, 1919.

Kawamata, Keiji [Shozo Chiba], adapt. "Nishonen no Boken." *Dowa* 4:4–10 (1923).

Sasaki, Kuni, trans. "Tom Sawyer." In *Mark Twain Meisaku Shu.* Tokyo: Kaizosha, 1929.

———. *Tom Sawyer no Boken.* Tokyo: Shunyodo, 1932.

Shibusawa, Seika, trans. *Tom Sawyer no Boken.* Tokyo: Bunka Shobo, 1933.

Ishida, Eiji, trans. *Tom Sawyer no Boken.* Tokyo: Iwanami Shoten, 1946.

Shibusawa, Seika, trans. *Tom Sawyer no Boken.* Tokyo: Dowa Shunjusha, 1947.

Koide, Shogo, trans. *Meisaku Monogatari: Tom Sawyer no Boken.* Tokyo: Kobunsha, 1948.

Sasaki, Kuni, trans. *Tom Sawyer no Boken.* Tokyo: Dainippon Yubenkai Kodansha, 1950.

Okubo, Yasuo, trans. *Tom Sawyer no Boken.* In *Sekai Bungaku Sensho,* vol. 93. Tokyo: Mikasa Shobo, 1951.

Ishii, Momoko, trans. *Tom Sawyer no Boken.* Tokyo: Iwanami Shoten, 1952.

Okubo, Yasuo, trans. *Tom Sawyer no Boken.* Tokyo: Shinchosha, 1952.

Sato, Rikichi, trans. *Tom Sawyer no Boken.* Tokyo: Kadokawa Shoten, 1952.

Hirai, Yoshio, trans. *Tom Sawyer no Boken.* Tokyo: Iwanami Shoten, 1962.

Toki, Yukio, trans. *Tom Sawyer no Boken.* In *Mark Twain Meisaku Zenshu,* vol. 3. Tokyo: Iwasaki Shoten, 1962.

Saito, Shoji, trans. *Tom Sawyer no Boken.* Tokyo: Kadokawa Shoten, 1964.

Shirayanagi, Yoshihiko, trans. *Tom Sawyer no Boken.* Tokyo: Jitsugyo no Nihonsha, 1976.

Sakashita, Noboru, trans. *Tom Sawyer no Boken.* Tokyo: Kodansha, 1978.

Kakinuma, Takako, trans. *Tom Sawyer no Boken.* Tokyo: Sairyusha, 1996.

A Tramp Abroad (1880)

Iizuka, Eiichi, Noboru Matsumoto, and Hitoshi Namekata, trans. *Yoroppa Horoki.* 2 vols. Tokyo: Sairyusha, 1996.

The Prince and the Pauper (1882)

Kawa, Sanjin [Kawasanjin Kawada], Sanjin Ko [Kosanjin Kuroda], and Sanjin Sazanami [Sazanami Iwaya], trans. "Kojiki Oji." *Shonen Sekai* 4:1–27 (January–December 1898).

———. *Shonen Shosetsu, Kojiki Oji.* Tokyo: Bunbudo, 1899.

Suzuki, Miekichi, trans. "Kojiki no Oji." *Akai Tori* 14:3–6, 15:1–5 (1925).

Muraoka, Hanako, trans. *Oji to Kojiki.* In *Sekai Katei Bungaku Taikei,* vol. 2. Tokyo: Heibonsha, 1927.

Kojima, Seijiro, trans. "Kojiki Oji." *Shonen Kurabu* (January–December 1930).

———. *Kojiki Oji.* Tokyo: Shunyodo, 1933.

Muraoka, Hanako, trans. *Oji to Kojiki.* Tokyo: Iwanami Shoten, 1934.

Osaragi, Jiro, adapt. "Hanamaru Kotorimaru." *Shonen Kurabu* 26:1–12 (1939).

———. *Hanamaru Kotorimaru.* Tokyo: Chuokoronsha, 1941.

———. *Hanamaru Kotorimaru.* Tokyo: Popurasha, 1952.

———. *Hanamaru Kotorimaru/Suishoyama no Shonen.* Tokyo: Kodansha, 1970.

Otaguro, Katsuhiko, trans. *Kojiki Oji.* Tokyo: Dainippon Yubenkai Kodansha, 1950.

Ishikawa, Jun, adapt. "Kojiki Oji." *Bungei* 9:8 (1952).

Terai, Yasuo, trans. *Oji to Kojiki.* Tokyo: Kadokawa Shoten, 1952.

Matsumoto, Keiko, trans. *Oji to Kojiki.* Tokyo: Shinchosha, 1954.

Yamamoto, Choichi, trans. *Oji to Kojiki.* Tokyo: Sairyusha, 1999.

Life on the Mississippi (1883)

Ueno, Naozo, trans. *Mississippi-gawa jo no Seikatsu.* Tokyo: Sogensha, 1948.

Shioya, Taro, trans. *Mississippi no Boken.* In *Mark Twain Meisaku Zenshu,* vol. 10. Tokyo: Iwasaki Shoten, 1962.

Katsuura, Yoshio, trans. *Mississippi-gawa jo no Seikatsu.* Tokyo: Bunka Shobo Hakubunsha, 1993.

Yoshida, Eiko, trans. *Mississippi no Seikatsu.* 2 vols. Tokyo: Sairyusha, 1994–1995.

Adventures of Huckleberry Finn (1885)

Sasaki, Kuni, trans. *Huckleberry Monogatari.* Tokyo: Seika Shoin, 1921.

———. *Huckleberry no Boken.* Tokyo: Shunyodo, 1932.

Nakamura, Tameji, trans. *Huckleberry Finn no Boken.* 2 vols. Tokyo: Iwanami Shoten, 1941.

Tatsunokuchi, Naotaro, trans. *Huckleberry Finn no Boken: Jiyu wo Motometa America Shonen.* Tokyo: Shin Shokokuminsha, 1948.

Tsutsui, Keisuke, trans. *Huckleberry no Boken.* Tokyo: Kisetsusha, 1948.

Koide, Shogo, trans. *Yadonashi Huck no Boken.* Tokyo: Kobunsha, 1950.

Ozaki, Shiro, trans. *Huckleberry no Boken.* Tokyo: Akane Shobo, 1951.

Sasaki, Kuni, trans. *Huckleberry no Boken.* Tokyo: Dainippon Yubenkai Kodansha, 1951.

Muraoka, Hanako, trans. *Huckleberry no Boken.* Tokyo: Shinchosha, 1959.

Shiraki, Shigeru, trans. *Huckleberry no Boken.* Tokyo: Iwanami Shoten, 1961.

———. *Huckleberry Finn no Boken.* In *Mark Twain Meisaku Zenshu,* vol. 2. Tokyo: Iwasaki Shoten, 1962.

Karita, Motoji, trans. *Huckleberry Finn no Boken.* Tokyo: Obunsha, 1969.

Nozaki, Takashi, trans. *Huckleberry Finn no Boken.* Tokyo: Kodansha, 1971.

Ishikawa, Kin'ichi, trans. "Huckleberry Finn no Boken." In *Chikuma Sekai Bungaku Taikei,* vol. 35. Tokyo: Chikuma Shobo, 1973.

Nishida, Minoru, trans. *Huckleberry Finn no Boken.* 2 vols. Tokyo: Iwanami Shoten, 1977.

Watanabe, Toshio, trans. "Huckleberry Finn no Boken." In *Mark Twain, Sekai Bungaku Zenshu,* vol. 54. Tokyo: Shueisha, 1980.

Yamamoto, Choichi, trans. *Huckleberry Finn no Boken.* Tokyo: Sairyusha, 1996.

Katsuura, Yoshio, trans. *Huckleberry Finn no Boken.* Tokyo: Bunkashobo Hakubunsha, 1998.

Okubo, Hiroshi, trans. *Huckleberry Finn no Boken.* Tokyo: Kadokawa Shoten, 1999.

Tatematsu, Wahei, trans. *Huckleberry Finn no Boken.* Tokyo: Kodansha, 1999.

Kajima, Shozo, trans. *Huckleberry Finn no Boken.* Tokyo: Chikuma Shobo, 2001.

A Connecticut Yankee in King Arthur's Court (1889)

Ogura, Takashi, trans. *Arthur-o Kyutei no Yankee.* Tokyo: Hayakawa Shobo, 1963.

Tatsunokuchi, Naotaro, trans. *Arthur-o Kyutei no Yankee.* Tokyo: Tokyo Sogensha, 1976.

Okubo, Hiroshi, trans. *Arthur-o Kyutei no Yankee.* Tokyo: Kadokawa Shoten, 1980.

———. *Hank Morgan no Boken.* Tokyo: Ronsosha, 1984.

Sunagawa, Hirokazu, trans. *Arthur-o Kyutei no Connecticut Yankee.* Tokyo: Sairyusha, 2000.

Tom Sawyer Abroad (1892)

Okubo, Yasuo, trans. *Tom Sawyer no Kuchu Ryoko.* Tokyo: Jitsugyo no Nihonsha, 1950.

Miyawaki, Norio, trans. "Tom Sawyer no Kuchu Ryoko." In *Mark Twain Meisaku Zenshu,* vol. 5. Tokyo: Iwasaki Shoten, 1962.

The American Claimant (1892)

Mikame, Masahiro, trans. *Amerika no Shakuiken Shuchosha.* Tokyo: Sairyusha, 1999.

Extracts from Adam's Diary (1893)

Honma, Hisashiro [Hisashi Honma], trans. *Adam no Nikki.* Tokyo: Bunrokudo Shoten, 1907.

Tatsunokuchi, Naotaro, trans. *Mark Twain: Adam no Nikki.* Tokyo: Yakumo Shoten, 1949.

"The £1,000,000 Bank-Note" (1893)

Nishikawa, Masami, trans. "Hyakuman Pondo no Shihei." In *America Shosetsu-sen.* Tokyo: Chikuma Shobo, 1951.

Ueno, Naozo, trans. "Hyakuman Pondo Shihei." In *Calaveras-gun no Nadakaki Tobigaeru, Kaibutsu.* Tokyo Nan'undo, 1960.

Furusawa, Yasujiro, trans. "Hyakuman Pondo Shihei." In *Mark Twain Tanpenshu.* Tokyo: Shinchosha, 1961.

Ueda, Tsutomu, trans. "Hyakuman Pondo Shihei." In *Sekai Tanpen Bungaku Zenshu, America Bungaku 19-seiki.* Tokyo: Shueisha, 1964.

Katsuura, Yoshio, trans. "Hyakuman Pondo Ginkoken." In *Mark Twain Tanpen Zenshu,* vol. 2. Tokyo: Bunka Shobo Hakubunsha, 1994.

"Is He Living or Is He Dead?" (1893)

Yamagata, Isoo, trans. "Seishi Ikan." *Shonen Bunko,* November 1893, 250–58.

Arishima, Takeo, adapt. "Domomata no Shi." *Izumi,* October 1922, 5–41.

Pudd'nhead Wilson and Those Extraordinary Twins (1894)

Sasaki, Kuni, trans. "Nuke Wilson." (Translation of *Pudd'nhead Wilson* only.) In *Mark Twain Meisaku-shu,* 8–200. Tokyo: Kaizosha, 1929.

Ueda, Kenjiro, trans. "Manuke Wilson no Katsuyaku." In *Mark Twain Meisaku Zenshu,* vol. 8. Tokyo: Iwasaki Shoten, 1962.

Nozaki, Takashi, trans. "Notarin Wilson no Higeki." In *Igirisu Meisakushu, America Meisakushu.* Tokyo: Chuokoron, 1966.

Murakawa, Takehiko, trans. *Manuke no Wilson to kano Ikei no Soseiji.* Tokyo: Sairyusha, 1994.

"Tom Sawyer, Detective" (1896)

Okubo, Yasuo, trans. *Meitantei Tom Sawyer.* Tokyo: Jitsugyo no Nihonsha, 1950.

———. *Meitantei Tom Sawyer.* Tokyo: Shinchosha, 1955.

———. *Tom Sawyer no Tantei Tanken.* Tokyo: Shinchosha, 1969.

Personal Recollections of Joan of Arc (1896)

Okubo, Hiroshi, trans. *Mark Twain no Joan of Arc: Joan of Arc ni tsuite no Kojinteki Kaiso.* Tokyo: Kadokawa Shoten, 1996.

Following the Equator (1897)

Iizuka, Eiichi, trans. *Sekido ni Sotte.* 2 vols. Tokyo: Sairyusha, 1999–2000.

"The Man That Corrupted Hadleyburg" (1899)

Furusawa, Yasujiro, trans. "Hadleyburg no Machi wo Fuhai Saseta Otoko." In *Mark Twain Tanpenshu.* Tokyo: Shinchosha, 1961.

Katsuura, Yoshio, trans. "Hadleyburg wo Daraku Saseta Otoko." In *Mark Twain Tanpen Zenshu,* vol. 2. Tokyo: Bunka Shobo Hakubunsha, 1994.

Eve's Diary (1906)

Tatsunokuchi, Naotaro, trans. *Eve no Nikki, hoka 5-hen.* Tokyo: Iwanami Shoten, 1952.
Okubo, Hiroshi, trans. *Adam to Eve no Nikki.* Tokyo: Obunsha, 1976.

What Is Man? (1906)

Momose, Fumio, and Tadashi Matsumoto, trans. *Nigen to wa Nanika?* Tokyo: Nan'undo, 1966.
Nakano, Yoshio, trans. *Ningen to wa Nanika?* Tokyo: Iwanami Shoten, 1973.
Yoshioka, Eiichi, and Miyuki Furuyama, trans. *Ningen to wa Nanika?* Tokyo: Sairyusha, 1995.

Mark Twain's Speeches (1910)

Kanaya, Yoshio, trans. *Mark Twain Speech Shu.* Tokyo: Sairyusha, 2001.

The Mysterious Stranger (ed. Albert Bigelow Paine and Frederick A. Duneka, New York: Harper and Brothers, 1923)

Nakano, Yoshio, trans. *Fushigina Shonen.* Tokyo: Iwanami Shoten, 1969.

Europe and Elsewhere (ed. Albert Bigelow Paine, New York: Harper and Brothers, 1923)

Nogawa, Hiromi, trans. *Chikyu Kiko.* Tokyo: Sairyusha, 2001.

The Love Letters of Mark Twain (ed. Dixon Wecter, New York: Harper and Brothers, 1949)

Nakagawa, Keiko, and Mitsuko Miyamoto, trans. *Mark Twain no Love Letter.* Tokyo: Sairyusha, 1999.

The Autobiography of Mark Twain (ed. Charles Neider, New York: Harper and Row, 1959)

Watanabe, Toshio, trans. *Mark Twain Jiden.* In *America Koten Bunko,* vol. 6. Tokyo: Kenkyusha, 1975.
Katsuura, Yoshio, trans. *Mark Twain Jiden.* 2 vols. Tokyo: Chikuma Shobo, 1984.

Letters from the Earth (ed. Bernard DeVoto, New York: Harper and Row, 1962)

Kakinuma, Takako, Eiichi Yoshioka, and Yutaka Sato, trans. *Chikyu kara no Tegami.* Tokyo: Sairyusha, 1995.

Mark Twain's Letters from Hawaii (ed. A. Grove Day, New York: Appleton-Century, 1966)

Okubo, Hiroshi, trans. *Chotto Omoshiroi Hawaii Tsushin.* Tokyo: Obunsha, 1983.
Yoshioka, Eiichi, Morio Sano, and Makoto Yasuoka, trans. *Hawaii Tsushin.* Tokyo: Sairyusha, 2000.

3,000 Years among the Microbes (ed. John S. Tuckey, in _Mark Twain's Which Was the Dream? and Other Symbolic Writings of the Later Years,_ Berkeley and Los Angeles: University of California Press, 1966)

Arima, Yoko, trans. *Saikin Huck no Boken.* Tokyo: Sairyusha, 1996.

No. 44, The Mysterious Stranger (ed. John S. Tuckey and William M. Gibson, Berkeley and Los Angeles: University of California Press, 1982)

Katsuura, Yoshio, trans. "Fushigina Wakamono." In *Mark Twain Tanpen Zenshu,* vol. 3. Tokyo: Bunka Shobo Hakubunsha, 1994.
Okubo, Hiroshi, trans. *Fushigina Shonen 44-go.* Tokyo: Kadokawa Shoten, 1994.

Yamamoto, Choichi, and Yutaka Sato, trans. *Mysterious Stranger 44-go.* Tokyo: Sairyusha, 1995.

Twain and His Works in Japanese School Textbooks

Susukida, Kyukin. "Sakusha wa Dareka." *In Chugaku Kokugo 1,* vol. 1, ed. Choji Nose, 50–51. Tokyo: Taishukan, 1949.

———. "Kumo." In *Atarashii Kokugo, Chugaku 2-nen,* vol. 1, ed. Kunio Yanagita, 41–42. Tokyo: Tokyo Shoseki, 1951.

———. "Enzetsu wo Nusumareta Hanashi." In *Shin Chugaku Kokugo 1,* vol. 1, ed. Choji Nose, 103–6. Tokyo: Taishukan, 1952.

———. "Enzetsu wo Nusumareta Hanashi." In *Shin Chugaku Kokugo 1,* vol. 1, ed. Choji Nose, 141–44. Tokyo: Taishukan, 1954.

———. "Shima." In *Chugaku Kokugo 1-nen,* vol. 2, ed. Zenmaro Toki, 163. Tokyo: Chukyo Shuppan, 1958.

———. "Enzetsu wo Nusumareta Hanashi." In *Chugakko Kokugo 1-nen,* vol. 2, ed. Naoya Shiga, 6–9. Tokyo: Gakko Tosho, 1962.

Ishida, Eiji, trans. "Hei wo Nuru Tom Sawyer," excerpted from *The Adventures of Tom Sawyer.* In *Chugaku Gendai Kokugo 2,* vol. 1, ed. Seijo Kokubungakkkai, 100–108. Tokyo: Ichigaya Shuppan, 1951.

———. "Jam to Kabutomushi," excerpted from *The Adventures of Tom Sawyer.* In *Atarashii Kokugo Chugaku 3-nen,* vol. 1, ed. Kunio Yanagita, 121–25. Tokyo: Tokyo Shoseki, 1954.

Mitsuyoshi, Natsuya, trans. "Hei wo Nuru Tom Sawyer," excerpted from *The Adventures of Tom Sawyer.* In *Chugaku Shin Kokugo 1,* vol. 1, ed. Sanseido Henshujo, 107–17. Tokyo: Sanseido, 1951.

"Jisho Yodan." In *Chuto Kokugo 1,* vol. 2, ed. Kyosuke Kindaichi et al., 25–27. Tokyo: Sanseido, 1952.

Yoshida, Kinetaro, trans. "Hei wo Nuru Tom Sawyer." In *Chugaku Shin Kokugo 1-nen,* ed. Haruo Sato, 11–25. Tokyo: Sanseido, 1957.

Tatsunokuchi, Naotaro, trans. "Huckleberry to Jim," excerpted from *Adventures of Huckleberry Finn.* In *Kokugo Sogo 3,* vol. 2, ed. Kagejiro Kazamaki, 35–44. Tokyo: Kairyudo, 1959.

Articles and Essays in Popular Magazines and Newspapers

1950s

"Gendai ni Ikiru Koten: Mark Twain no Adam, Eve no Nikki." *Asahi Shimbun,* September 20, 1957, sec. 6.
Newspaper article on the Japanese translations of *Extracts from Adam's Diary* and *Eve's Diary.*

"Mark Twain no Boken no Shogai." *Reader's Digest,* Japanese ed., March 1958, 126–75.
Translation of a *Reader's Digest* summary of Jerry Allen's biography *Adventures of Mark Twain* (Boston: Little, Brown, 1954).

1960s

"Osorubeki Totetsu-ryoku: Mark Twain Botsugo 50-nen." *Asahi Journal,* June 26, 1960, 44.
Overview of the American reception of Twain's works in the fifty years after his death.

1970s

Masui, Keisuke. "Mark Twain no Kurai Jinseikan." *Asahi Shimbun,* March 31, 1970, evening ed., Arts sec.
Newspaper article on Twain's pessimistic philosophy in his later days.

"M. Twain no Mihappyo *Tegami-shu.*" *Asahi Shimbun,* June 29, 1970, evening ed.
Short newspaper article reporting the discovery of Twain's letters in America.

"Mark Twain no Tegami ga Kyuhyaku-man'en." *Tokyo Shimbun,* August 7, 1970, evening ed.
Newspaper article on the discovery of Twain's letters in America and the high bidding on those letters.

"Eiga Tom Sawyer no Boken ga Dekirumade." *Reader's Digest,* Japanese ed., July 1973, 68–75.

Translation of a *Reader's Digest* article on the film *Mark Twain's Tom Sawyer,* dir. Don Taylor, United Artists–Reader's Digest, 1973.

"Tom Sawyer wo Kaita Hito." *Reader's Digest,* Japanese ed., September 1973, 180–224.

Translation of a bibliographical sketch about Twain.

Kamei, Shunsuke. "Bunmei Hihyo to Ningen no Tanoshisa Afureru." *Shukan Bunshun,* October 13, 1977, 114.

Review of a reprint of *Akagetto Gaiyuki* (The innocents abroad), trans. Seijiro Hamada. The reviewer emphasizes the balance Twain achieved between social criticism and humor in this work.

1980s

"Mark Twain Saigo no Sakuhin: Fushigina Tabibito 44-go." *Yomiuri Shimbun,* February 11, 1983.

Newspaper article on the publication of *No. 44, The Mysterious Stranger* in America. Includes a discussion of Albert Bigelow Paine's deceptive alteration of Twain's manuscript in 1916.

"Tsurumi Shunsuke-san to Tom Sawyer wo Yomu." *Asahi Shimbun,* May 20, 1984, sec. 12.

Newspaper article quoting Shunsuke Tsurumi, a leading Japanese philosopher, on *Tom Sawyer.* Tsurumi argues for the significance of Tom's critical view of adults and expresses concern about modern Japanese children who seem to be too busy to develop their own critical views.

Ayukawa, Nobuo. "Jidai wo Yomu: *Mark Twain Jiden.*" *Shukan Bunshun,* December 6, 1984, 154.

Magazine article discussing Twain's philosophy and life and introducing Yoshio Katsuura's translation of *The Autobiography of Mark Twain.*

Shiba, Ryotaro. "Toyo to Seiyo no Hazamade: Uttaeru beki Aite ga Naimama." *Shukan Asahi,* January 4–11, 1985, 68–77.

Long magazine essay by one of the most popular and acclaimed Japanese writers of the late twentieth century. A critical examination of late twentieth-century Japanese society, with references to Twain's pessimistic philosophy and Buddhist philosophy.

"Jinshu Sabetsu Shugisha? Utagai Harasu Shokan Hakken: Meiyo wo Kaifuku shita Twain." *Yomiuri Shimbun,* March 18, 1985, evening ed., sec. 9.

Newspaper article reporting the discovery of a letter in which Twain offered financial help to a black student at Yale Law School. The article suggests that this discovery might help to dispel the charge that Twain was racist.

"Twain no Omei Sosogu Hakken." *Asahi Shimbun,* May 4, 1985, evening ed., sec. 9.

Newspaper article with almost the same content as the article listed above.

Kamei, Shunsuke. "Hyakusai no Akudo Huckleberry Finn." *Chuo Koron,* June 1985, 157–69.

Centennial review of *Adventures of Huckleberry Finn* by a leading Japanese Twain scholar.

"*Tom Sawyer no Boken:* Taberu Kotoni Isshokenmeni." *Asahi Shimbun,* July 23, 1985, sec. 13.

Newspaper article about the variety of descriptions of food in *The Adventures of Tom Sawyer.*

Yamaguchi, Masao. "Shinwateki Sekai to shite no *Huckleberry Finn.*" *Kikan Hermes,* March 1986, 211–23.

Another centennial review of *Adventures of Huckleberry Finn,* this one by a leading Japanese anthropologist.

"Twain no Sugao." *Asahi Shimbun,* November 3, 1986, sec. 7.

Newspaper article on the discovery of an unpublished manuscript by Twain in the Mark Twain Project of the University of California at Berkeley.

"Twain no Isaku wo Kokyo no Dojinshi Hatsu Keisai." *Asahi Shimbun,* February 23, 1987, sec. 7, evening ed.

Newspaper article on the publication in the *Missouri Review* of an unpublished short story by Twain.

Kamizaki, Rin'ichi. "Money Bungaku Sanpo, Tom Sawyer no Boken: 1-man doru to Doshin." *Mainichi Shimbun,* June 22, 1987, evening ed.

Newspaper article on the relationship between money and *The Adventures of Tom Sawyer.*

"Mark Twain no 'Yo wa Hawaii wo Hakken seri.'" Trans. Ryuichi Ohka, illus. Norihisa Tojinbara. *Esquire,* Japanese ed., July 1988, 55–61.

Translation of Twain's report on life and culture in Hawaii, which appeared in *Roughing It.*

Kamei, Shunsuke. "Showa, Heisei 'Kinpika Jidai' no Seishin." *Bungei Shunju,* September 1989, 94–105.

This magazine essay on the superficiality of contemporary Japanese society refers to Twain and American society of the Gilded Age.

"Bokura no Tom Sawyer Taiken: Iede no Omoide." *Shukan Hoseki,* September 28, 1989, 102–3.

This magazine article uses Tom Sawyer's escape from home to introduce some well-known Japanese people's recollections of escaping from home.

1990s

Anno Mitsumasa. "Suisu no Tani, Mark Twain." Illus. Anno Mitsumasa. *Asahi Graph,* January 19, 1990, 82–83.

With some beautiful illustrations of the Alps, this magazine essay introduces Twain's humorous stories about his visits to the Alps in *A Tramp Abroad.*

Kihara, Buichi. "Sekai Bungaku High Vision 28: Mark Twain, Huckleberry Finn no Boken." *Shukan Shincho,* October 11, 1990, 94–98.

Magazine essay recounting the main events and story line of *Adventures of Huckleberry Finn.*

Ikeuchi, Osamu. "Oji to Kojiki, Shonen Tankentai 9." *Gekkan Hyakka,* March 1991, 36–39.

Brief magazine essay on *The Prince and the Pauper* by a leading Japanese scholar of American literature.

Gates, David. "Mark Twain mo Bikkuri: Beibungakkai wo Daironso ni Makikonda Shinsaku, *Huck wa Kokujin datta?*" *Newsweek,* Japanese ed., August 6, 1992, 50–52.

Translation of a prepublication review of Shelley Fisher Fishkin's *Was Huck Black? Mark Twain and African American Voices.*

"Ano Mark Twain ni Kosho Porno ga Atta!" *Jiyujikan,* February 1993, 31.

Magazine essay introducing Twain's *1601,* calling it "hilarious porno!"

McDonell, Terry. "Kaku Sogu Einstein to Mark Twain." *Esquire,* Japanese ed., December 1993, 44–46.

Translation of "1906 San Francisco: Collaboration of Twain and Einstein," a fictional story about a meeting between the two men.

Halloran, Fumiko. "Sakkatachi no Minami Taiheiyo: Mark Twain kara Ikezawa Natsuki made." *Chuo Koron,* March 1994, 308–20. Magazine piece introducing Twain's essays on Hawaii, in particular his criticism of American missionaries who destroyed the native culture.

Iwamoto, Iwao. "Shoshin Shomei no Twain no Isaku." Review of *Fushigi na Shonen 44-go,* trans. by Hiroshi Okubo. *Sunday Mainichi,* September 11, 1994, 113.

A leading Japanese scholar's brief review of Hiroshi Okubo's translation of *No. 44, The Mysterious Stranger.*

Horiuchi, Masami. "Omoide no Hon: Imadani *Tom Sawyer no Boken.*" *Shukan Bunshun,* September 15, 1994, 119.

A famous Japanese actor's brief recollection of reading *The Adventures of Tom Sawyer* in childhood.

Iwamoto, Iwao. "Kyokou wo Enjitsuzuketa Twain." *Sunday Mainichi,* December 24, 1995, 118.

A favorable review of Shunsuke Kamei's biographical study of Twain, *Mark Twain no Sekai* (The world of Mark Twain).

Tsuji, Masao. "Soshite Tom Sawyer ga." *Asahi Shimbun,* December 1, 1996, sec. 40.

A short nostalgic poem about *Tom Sawyer.*

Takahashi, Yoshito. Review of *Mark Twain no Joan of Arc,* trans. Hiroshi Okubo. *Sunday Mainichi,* January 26, 1997, 75–76.

A brief review of the first Japanese translation of *Personal Recollections of Joan of Arc.*

2000 and After

Hasebe, Fumichika. "Mark Twain, Huckleberry Finn no Boken: Kinsho Atsukai wo Uketahodo ni Jiyujizai na Sosaku." *Hato yo!* April 2000, 162–68.
A well-balanced magazine essay on *Adventures of Huckleberry Finn* with background information on the writing of the novel and a discussion of the novel's legacy in twentieth-century Japan and America.

Koyano, Atsushi. "Good Bad Boy no Keifu: Tom Sawyer no Boken." *Eureka,* February 2001, 39–47.
Magazine essay that critically examines *The Adventures of Tom Sawyer* with reference to a variety of twentieth-century Japanese "good/bad boy stories." Koyano also compares Twain with several Japanese novelists in the twentieth century.

"Wanpaku Kozo no Omokage wo Sagashini: Mississippi Gawa, Amerika Kindai Bungaku no Gensen wo Unda Oinaru 'Mizu no Chichi' wo Huck to Issho ni Kudaru." *Newsweek,* Japanese ed., May 5–9, 2001, 62–64.
A report on present-day Hannibal, Missouri, with a variety of colorful pictures.

Nagayama, Yasuo. "Nazotoki Shonen Shojo Sekai no Meisaku Dai-2-kai: *Oji to Kojiki.*" *Shincho 45,* February 2002, 200–204.
This magazine essay suggests that *The Prince and the Pauper* is a typical American story because of its anticlass views.

Nagai, Akira. "*Huckleberry Finn no Boken.*" *Asahi Shimbun,* February 24, 2002, sec. 4.
A brief recollection of the author's reading of *Adventures of Huckleberry Finn* in his childhood. Nagai says that he was amazed by the tremendous scale of Huck's adventures, compared with the tiny adventures Nagai played at when he was a child.

"Te ga Utau, Oto ga Mieru." *Asahi Shimbun,* September 21, 2004, sec. 31.
An anonymous introduction to the musical *Big River.*

Nishikawa, Nobuhiro. "Rousha to Chousha no Kizuna ni Yuki to Kibou." *Asahi Shimbun,* October 7, 2004, sec. 32.
A favorable review of the musical *Big River.*

Films

For non-Twain Japanese films, U.S. films, and U.S. versions of Japanese animes, see bibliography.

Japanese Film and Animated Adaptations

Hanamaru Kotorimaru. Film adapt. of *The Prince and the Pauper.* Dir. Shinzo Yoshida. Shinko Kyoto Film, 1941.

Huckleberry Finn no Boken. Animated adapt. of *Adventures of Huckleberry Finn.* 26 episodes. Group Tack, Fuji Television Network, January 1–June 25, 1976. Scenario at Art Research Center, Ritsumeikan University, Kyoto.

"Kikakusho Kogai (Proposal and Summary)." Art Research Center, no. S-04556.

"Tabi no Odoroki." Art Research Center, no. S-23852.

"Tabi no Odoroki." Rev. version. Art Research Center, no. S-16316.

Tom Sawyer no Boken. Animated adapt. of *The Adventures of Tom Sawyer.* Dir. Hiroshi Saito, prod. Takaji Matsudo, scen. Akira Miyazaki. 49 episodes. Nippon Animation, Fuji Television Network, January 6–December 28, 1980.

Huckleberry Finn Monogatari. Animated adapt. of *Adventures of Huckleberry Finn.* Dir. Norio Kashima, prod. Yoshinori Enoki. 26 episodes. Enoki Films, NHK BS2, August 26, 1994–March 3, 1995.

U.S. Films Distributed in Japan and Contemporary Reviews

1922 *Chame Kozo* (Huckleberry Finn). Dir. William Desmond Taylor, Paramount, 1920, distributed in Japan by Nikkatsu Yunyu.

"Huckleberry Finn." *Kinema Junpo,* September 11, 1922, 5–6.

"Chame Kozo." *Kinema Junpo,* October 11, 1922, 14.

1931 *Tom Sawyer no Boken* (The adventures of Tom Sawyer). Dir. John Cromwell, Paramount, 1930, distributed by the Japanese branch of Paramount.

Shimizu, Chiyota. "Tom Sawyer no Boken." *Kinema Junpo,* January 1, 1931, 76–77.

"Tom Sawyer no Boken." *Kinema Junpo,* January 11, 1931, 23–24.
Iijima, Tadashi. "Tom Sawyer no Boken." *Kinema Junpo,* April 1, 1931, 79.
Advertisements in *Kinema Junpo*: December 11, 1930, February 11 (p. 162), March 1, 1931.

1931 *Yukai na Bushido* (A Connecticut yankee in King Arthur's court). Dir. David Butler, with Will Rogers, Fox, 1931, distributed by Japanese branch of Fox.
Shimizu, Chiyota. "Yukai na Bushido." *Kinema Junpo,* May 1, 1931, 52.
"Yukai na Bushido." *Kinema Junpo,* May 11, 1931, 36.
"Yukai na Bushido." *Kinema Junpo,* July 21, 1931, 31.
Advertisements in *Kinema Junpo*: April 21, May 1, 11, 21, June 1, 1931.

1932 *Wanpaku Taisho* (Huckleberry Finn). Dir. Norman Taurog, Paramount, 1920, distributed by Japanese branch of Paramount.
"Wanpaku Taisho." *Kinema Junpo,* December 11, 1931, 28.
Shimizu, Chiyota. "Wanpaku Taisho." *Kinema Junpo,* January 1, 1932, 69.
Iijima, Tadashi. "Wanpaku Taisho." *Kinema Junpo,* January 21, 1932, 44.
Advertisements in *Kinema Junpo*: November 11, December 1, 11 (p. 90), January 1, 11, 1932.

1949 *Yadonashi Huck no Boken* (The adventures of Huckleberry Finn). Dir. Richard Thorpe, with Mickey Rooney, MGM, 1939.
"Yadonashi Huck no Boken." *Kinema Junpo* 67 (October 1949), 30.
Shimizu, Akira. "Yadonashi Huck no Boken." *Kinema Junpo* 67 (October 1949), 35.

1950 *Horo no Oji* (The prince and the pauper). Dir. William Keighley, Warner Brothers, 1937.
"Horo no Oji." *Kinema Junpo* 77 (March 1950), 40.

1951 *Tom Sawyer no Boken* (The adventures of Tom Sawyer). Dir. Norman Taurog, United Artists, 1938, distributed by Toho Yoga-bu.
"Tom Sawyer no Boken." *Kinema Junpo,* July 1, 1951, 101.
Advertisements in *Kinema Junpo*: June 15, July 1, 1951.

1954 *Harukaze to Hyakuman Shihei* (Man with a million; adapt. of

"The £1,000,000 Bank-Note"). Dir. Ronald Neame, with Gregory Peck, United Artists, 1954, distributed by Shochiku.

Shimizu, Shunji. "Harukaze to Hyakuman Shihei." *Kinema Junpo* 89 (April 1954), 44–45.

"Harukaze to Hyakuman Shihei." *Kinema Junpo* 89 (April 1954), 121–22.

"Yoki Jidai no Kaiso: Harukaze to Hyakuman Shihei." *Asahi Shimbun,* April 15, 1954, sec. 2.

Advertisements in *Kinema Junpo* 89 (April 1954), *Kinema Junpo* 90 (May 1, 1954).

1973 *Tom Sawyer no Boken* (Mark Twain's Tom Sawyer). Dir. Don Taylor, United Artists–Reader's Digest, 1973.

"Tom Sawyer no Boken to Amerikanism no Sekai." *Kinema Junpo* 608 (July 1973), feature review, no page number.

Ono, Kosei. "Tom Sawyer no Boken to Amerikanism no Sekai." *Kinema Junpo* 608 (July 1973), 62–69.

Fukuoka, Tsubasa. "Yoji Taiken no Saikakunin to Jiko Kensho: Tom Sawyer no Boken." *Kinema Junpo* 608 (July 1973), 135–36.

"Tom Sawyer no Boken." *Kinema Junpo* 610 (August 1973), 174–75.

"Sengo Hatsu no Tojo, Tom Sawyer no Boken: Shinsen de Kokoro Atatamaru Eiga." *Asahi Shimbun,* August 1, 1973, sec. 9, evening ed.

Stage Productions

Adventure Musical Tom Sawyer. Dir. Masaaki Osumi, with Shinobu Sakagami, July–August 1987.

Musical adaptation of *The Adventures of Tom Sawyer* featuring popular young actors.

Big River. Dir. Michael Greif, prod. Saburo Kitamura, music by Roger Miller, trans. Yoji Aoi, with Hiroyuki Sanada and Ron Richardson. Aoyama Theater, Tokyo, March 4–May 5, 1988, Kintetsu Theater, Osaka, May 10–29, 1988.

The Japanese version of the Tony award–winning musical

based on *Adventures of Huckleberry Finn.* Hiroyuki Sanada played Huck and Ron Richardson played Jim, the role he originated on Broadway.

Big River. Dir. Jeff Calhoun, with Tyrone Giordano and Michael McElroy, presented by the Deaf West Theater, Aoyama Theater, Tokyo, September 28–October 24, 2004.
A revival of *Big River* performed by deaf, hard-of-hearing, and hearing actors.

Aro Aro Camelot? Dir. Tetsunori Ota, with Takarazuka Kagekidan Hanagumi, Takarazuka Bau Hall, Osaka, May 29–June 12, 1994.
A musical adaptation of *A Connecticut Yankee in King Arthur's Court* by the all-female musical group Takarazuka-kagekidan.

Bibliography

Books and Articles

In English

Aldrich, Thomas Bailey. *The Story of a Bad Boy.* Boston: Fields Osgood, 1869.

Appadurai, Arjun. "Disjuncture and Difference in the Global Cultural Economy." *Public Culture* 2:2 (1990): 1–24.

Arac, Jonathan. *Huckleberry Finn as Idol and Target: The Functions of Criticism in Our Time.* Madison: University of Wisconsin Press, 1997.

Asselineau, Roger. *The Literary Reputation of Mark Twain from 1910 to 1950: A Critical Essay and a Bibliography.* Paris: Librairie Marcel Dider, 1954.

Atkins, Taylor. *Blue Nippon: Authenticating Jazz in Japan.* Durham, NC: Duke University Press, 2001.

Blair, Walter. *Mark Twain and Huck Finn.* Berkeley and Los Angeles: University of California Press, 1960.

Budd, Louis J. "Mark Twain as an American Icon." In *The Cambridge Companion to Mark Twain,* ed. Forrest G. Robinson, 1–26. New York: Cambridge University Press, 1995.

———. *Our Mark Twain: The Making of His Public Personality.* Philadelphia: University of Pennsylvania Press, 1983.

Camfield, Gregg. *Sentimental Twain: Samuel Clemens in the Maze of Moral Philosophy.* Philadelphia: University of Pennsylvania Press, 1994.

Cather, Willa. "A Tribute to Mark Twain." *Mark Twain Journal* 17:1 (1973–1974), back cover.

Cell, John W. *The Highest Stage of White Supremacy: The Origins of Segregation in South Africa and the American South.* Cambridge: Cambridge University Press, 1982.

Cohn, Joel R. *Studies in the Comic Spirit in Modern Japanese Fiction.* Cambridge, MA: Harvard University Press, 1998.

Condry, Ian. "Japanese Rap Music: An Ethnography of Globalization in Popular Culture." Ph.D. diss., Yale University, 1999.

DeVoto, Bernard. *Mark Twain's America.* Boston: Little, Brown, 1932.

Dower, John. *Embracing Defeat: Japan in the Wake of World War II.* New York: W.W. Norton, 1999.

———. *War without Mercy.* New York: Pantheon Books, 1986.

Eggleston, Edward. *The Hoosier Schoolmaster.* New York: Scribner, 1893.

Emerson, Everett. Afterword to *The Prince and the Pauper,* by Mark Twain. New York: Oxford University Press, 1996.

Fehrenbach, Heide, and Uta G. Poiger, eds. *Transactions, Transgressions, Transformations: American Culture in Western Europe and Japan.* New York: Berghahn Books, 2000.

Fishkin, Shelley Fisher. "In Praise of 'Spike Lee's Huckleberry Finn' by Ralph Wiley." *Mark Twain Circular* 13:4 (October–December 1999): 1–9.

———. *Lighting Out for the Territory: Reflections on Mark Twain and American Culture.* New York: Oxford University Press, 1996.

———. "Mark Twain in Japan." *South Atlantic Review* 65:4 (Fall 2000): 5–12.

———. "New Perspectives on 'Jim' in the 1990s." *Mark Twain Review (Korea),* Winter 1999: 5–19.

———. *Was Huck Black? Mark Twain and African-American Voices.* New York: Oxford University Press, 1993.

Frank, Perry June. "*Adventures of Huckleberry Finn* on Film." In *Huck Finn among the Critics: A Centennial Selection,* ed. Thomas Inge, 271–91. Frederick, MD: University Publications of America, 1985.

———. "*The Adventures of Tom Sawyer* on Film: The Evolution of an American Icon." Ph.D. diss., George Washington University, 1991.

Gordon, Jan B. "Fan-Tods 'wid' de Samurai: *Huckleberry Finn* in Japan." In *One Hundred Years of Huckleberry Finn: The Boy, His Book, and American Culture,* ed. Robert Sattelmeyer and J. Donald Crowley, 282–96. Columbia: University of Missouri Press, 1985.

Goto, Shoji. "Huck Finn and America in Kenzaburo Oe." In *Postmodernity and Cross-Culturalism,* ed. Yoshinobu Hakutani, 31–42. Madison, WI: Associated University Press, 2002.

Harris, George Washington. *Sut Lovingood: Yarns Spun by a "Nat'ral Born Durn'd Fool."* New York: Dick and Fitzgerald, 1867.

Haupt, Clyde V. *Huckleberry Finn on Film: Film and Television Adaptations of Mark Twain's Novel, 1920–1993.* Jefferson, NC: McFarland, 1994.

Hemingway, Ernest. *Green Hills of Africa.* New York: Scribner's, 1935.

Hirano, Kyoko. *Mr. Smith Goes to Tokyo: Japanese Cinema under the American Occupation, 1945–1952.* Washington, DC: Smithsonian Institution Press, 1992.

Howells, William Dean. *A Boy's Town.* New York: Harper and Brothers, 1890.

Kamei, Shunsuke. "Mark Twain in Japan." *Mark Twain Journal* 12:2 (Spring 1963): 10–11.

———. "Mark Twain in Japan, Reconsidered." In *Crosscurrents in the Literatures of Asia and the West,* ed. Masayuki Akiyama and Yiu-nam Leung, 73–81. Newark: University of Delaware Press, 1997.

Kaplan, Amy, and Donald E. Pease, eds. *Cultures of United States Imperialism.* Durham, NC: Duke University Press, 1993.

Krauth, Leland, "Mark Twain: The Victorian of Southwestern Humor." *American Literature* 54:3 (1982): 368–84.

———. *Proper Mark Twain.* Athens: University of Georgia Press, 1999.

Kuisel, Richard. *Seducing the French: The Dilemma of Americanization.* Berkeley and Los Angeles: University of California Press, 1993.

Kuwahara, Yasue. "Japanese Culture and Popular Consciousness: Disney's *The Lion King* vs. Tezuka's *Jungle Emperor.*" *Journal of Popular Culture* 31:1 (Summer 1997): 37–48.

Litwack, Leon. *Trouble in Mind: Black Southerners in the Age of Jim Crow.* New York: Knopf, 1998.

Lowell, James Russell. *The Biglow Papers: Second Series.* Boston: Ticknor and Fields, 1867.

Lynn, Kenneth. *Mark Twain and Southwestern Humor.* Boston: Little, Brown, 1959.

MacLeod, Anne Scott. *American Childhood: Essays on Children's Literature.* Athens: University of Georgia Press, 1994.

Marx, Leo. "Mr. Eliot, Mr. Trilling, and Huckleberry Finn," *American Scholar* 22:4 (Autumn 1953): 423–40.

———. *The Pilot and the Passenger: Essays on Literature, Technology, and Culture in the United States.* New York: Oxford University Press, 1988.

Miyoshi, Masao. *As We Saw Them: The First Japanese Embassy to the United States.* Berkeley and Los Angeles: University of California Press, 1979.

Napier, Susan J. *Anime from* Akira *to* Princess Mononoke*: Experiencing Contemporary Japanese Animation.* New York: Palgrave, 2000.

Nathan, John. Introduction to *Teach Us to Outgrow Our Madness: Four Short Novels by Kenzaburo Oe,* trans. John Nathan. New York: Grove Press, 1977.

Neider, Charles, ed. *Adventures of Huckleberry Finn,* by Samuel L. Clemens. Garden City, NY: Doubleday, 1985.

Nitobe, Inazo. *Bushido, the Soul of Japan: An Exposition of Japanese Thought.* Philadelphia: Leeds and Biddle, 1899, 1900.

Notoji, Masako. "Cultural Transformation of John Philip Sousa and Disneyland in Japan." In *"Here, There, and Everywhere": The Foreign Politics of American Popular Culture,* ed. Reinhold Wagnleitner and Elaine Tyler May, 219–26. Hanover, NH: University Press of New England, 2000.

Peck, George W. *Peck's Bad Boy and His Pa.* Chicago: Belford Clarke, 1883.

Pells, Richard. *Not Like Us: How Europeans Have Loved, Hated, and Transformed American Culture since World War II.* New York: Basic Books, 1997.

Poiger, Uta G. "Beyond 'Modernization' and 'Colonization.'" *Diplomatic History* 23:1 (1999): 45–56.

Quirk, Tom. *Coming to Grips with Huckleberry Finn: Essays on a Book, a Boy, and a Man.* Columbia: University of Missouri Press, 1993.

———. *Mark Twain: A Study of the Short Fiction.* New York: Twayne Publishers, 1997.

Raz, Aviad E. *Riding the Black Ship: Japan and Tokyo Disneyland.* Cambridge, MA: Harvard University Press, 1999.

Rodney, Robert M. *Mark Twain International: A Bibliography and Interpretation of His Worldwide Popularity.* Westport, CT: Greenwood Press, 1986.

Rubin, Jay. "From Wholesomeness to Decadence: The Censorship of Literature under the Allied Occupation." *Journal of Japanese Studies* 2:1 (1985): 71–103.

Russell, John G. "Consuming Passions: Spectacle, Self-Transformation, and the Commodification of Blackness in Japan." *Positions* 6:1 (1988): 113–77.

Sattelmeyer, Robert, and J. Donald Crowley, eds. *One Hundred Years of Huckleberry Finn: The Boy, His Book, and American Culture.* Columbia: University of Missouri Press, 1985.

Seelye, John. *The True Adventures of Huckleberry Finn.* Evanston, IL: Northwestern University Press, 1970.

Shillaber, Benjamin P. *Ike Partington and His Friends.* Boston: Lee and Shepard, 1878.

Smith, Henry Nash. *Mark Twain: The Development of a Writer.* Cambridge, MA: Harvard University Press, 1962.

Stam, Robert. "Beyond Fidelity." In *Film Adaptation,* ed. James Naremore, 54–76. New Brunswick, NJ: Rutgers University Press, 2000.

Stein, Ruth. "The A B C's of Counterfeit Classics: Adapted, Bowdlerized, and Condensed." *English Journal* 55 (December 1966): 1160–63.

Stone, Albert E. *The Innocent Eye: Childhood in Mark Twain's Imagination.* New Haven, CT: Yale University Press, 1961.

Tanizaki, Jun'ichiro. *Childhood Years: A Memoir.* Trans. Paul McCarthy. New York: Kodansha International, 1988.

Twain, Mark. *Adventures of Huckleberry Finn.* 1885. Reprint, New York: Oxford University Press, 1996.

———. *The Adventures of Tom Sawyer.* 1876. Reprint, New York: Oxford University Press, 1996.

———. *Is He Dead? A Comedy in Three Acts,* ed. Shelley Fisher Fishkin. Berkeley and Los Angeles: University of California Press, 2003.

———. *Life on the Mississippi.* 1883. Reprint, New York: Oxford University Press, 1996.

———. *The Prince and the Pauper.* 1882. Reprint, New York: Oxford University Press, 1996.

———. *Tom Sawyer Abroad.* 1894. Reprint, New York: Oxford University Press, 1996.

———. "Tom Sawyer, Detective." 1896. In *The Stolen White Elephant and Other Detective Stories.* New York: Oxford University Press, 1996.

———. *A Tramp Abroad.* 1880. Reprint, New York: Oxford University Press, 1996.

———. "A True Story, Repeated Word for Word as I Heard It." *Atlantic Monthly* 34:205 (1874): 591–94.

Victor, Metta Victoria Fuller. *A Bad Boy's Diary.* New York: J. S. Ogilvie, 1880.

———. *A Good Boy's Diary.* New York: G. W. Carleton, 1885.

———. *A Naughty Girl's Diary.* New York: G. W. Carleton, 1884.

Wagnleitner, Reinhold. *Coca-Colonization and the Cold War: The Cultural Mission of the United States in Austria after the Second World War.* Trans. Diana W. Wolf. Chapel Hill: University of North Carolina Press, 1994.

Wagnleitner, Reinhold, and Elaine Tyler May, eds. *"Here, There, and Everywhere": the Foreign Politics of American Popular Culture.* Hanover, NH: University Press of New England, 2000.

Warner, Charles Dudley. *Being a Boy.* Boston: J. R. Osgood, 1878.

Webster, Samuel Charles, ed. *Mark Twain, Business Man.* Boston: Little, Brown, 1946.

Woodward, C. Vann. *The Strange Career of Jim Crow.* Third rev. ed. New York: Oxford University Press, 1974.

In Japanese

Ando, Mikio. "Dokusha no Keisei/Sakusha no Keisei." In *Jido Bungaku to Shakai: Hokoku to Shinpojiumu,* ed. Teruo Jingu, 66–97. Tokyo: Meiji Shoin, 1974.

———. "Kindai Nihon Jido Bungaku no Houhou to Ningen-zou." In *Nihon Jido Bungaku no Tokushoku,* ed. Teruo Jingu et al., 185–221. Tokyo: Meiji Shoin, 1974.

Ando, Mikio, Yuhi Takezaki, Yasue Miyagawa, and Masako Shimizu. "Mark Twain kara Nani wo Uketsugu ka." *Nihon Jido Bungaku* 23:5 (1977): 20–43.

Arima, Yoko. *Mark Twain Shinkenkyu: Yume to Ban'nen no Fantasy.* Tokyo: Sairyusha, 2002.

Chiba, Shozo. "Tora-chan Nikki." *Dowa,* September–October 1925.

Economic Planning Agency. "Hataraku Josei: Atarashii Shakai Shisutemu wo Motomete." In *Heisei 9-nen Kokumin Seikatsu Hakusho.* Tokyo: Government Printing Office, 1997.

Eguchi, Sueyoshi. "Kyokasho Shuppan no Jiyu ni Tsuite." *Nihon Jido Bungaku* 16:8 (August 1970): 16–23.

Ezaki, Jun. "Bungaku Hokokukai Kessei made: *Bungei Nenkan* ni Miru Bungei Tosei." *Minshu Bungaku* 232 (March 1985): 96–103.

Fukuda, Yutaka. "Mittsu no Uncle Tom Monogatari." *Seikatsu Gakko* 3:8 (1948): 22–25.

Fukushima, Koichi. *Osaragi Jiro.* 2 vols. Tokyo: Soshisha, 1995.

Furuya, Tsunatake. "Jido Bungaku e no Yobo." *Jido* (July 1947): 14–19.

Hara, Sho. "Chiba Shozo Dowa-ron: Shozo to Twain wo Chushin ni." *Nihon Jido Bungaku* 22:2 (1976): 82–89.

Harada, Munenori. *Heisei Tom Sawyer.* Tokyo: Shueisha, 1998.

Hatakeyama, Choko. "'Monogatari Kankyo' toshite no Televi Animation." *Nihon Jido Bungaku* 41:2 (February 1995): 26–34.

Hatakeyama, Choko, and Masako Matsuyama. *Media Bunka to "Monogatari Kyoju": Shikakerareta Televi Animation.* Tokyo: Nire Shuppan, 1993.

———. *Monogatari no Hoso Keitairon: Shikakerareta Animation Bangumi.* Kyoto: Sekai Shisosha, 2000.

Hatanaka, Shigeo. *Nihon Fascism no Genron Dan'atsu Shoshi: Yokohama Jiken, Fuyu no Jidai no Shuppan Dan'atsu.* Tokyo: Kobunken, 1986.

Hayashi, Fumiko. "Furoji." *Bungei Shunju* 24:8 (1946): 66–72.

Hirano, Kyoko. *Tenno to Seppun: America Senryoka no Nihon Eiga Ken'etsu.* Trans. of *Mr. Smith Goes to Washington: Japanese Cinema under the American Occupation, 1945–1952,* by Kyoko Hirano. Tokyo: Soshisha, 1998.

Hirata, Shinsaku. "Nihon Moshi Tatakawaba!" *Shonen Kurabu,* May 1932, 82–93.

———. "Showa Yugeki–tai." *Shonen Kurabu,* January–December, 1934.

Horibe, Isao. "*Itazura Kozo Nikki* no Gensho." *Doshisha Kokubungaku* 35 (1991): 92–103.

Imae, Yoshitomo. "Nihongo to Jido Bungaku." In *Nihon Jido Bungaku no Tokushoku,* ed. Teruo Jingu et al., 50–87. Tokyo: Meiji Shoin, 1974.

Inoue, Teruko, and Yumiko Ehara, eds. *Josei no Data Book.* 3rd ed. Tokyo: Yuhikaku, 1999.

Ishida, Hitoshi. "Yugamerareta Tom Sawyer no Hon'yaku." *Seikatsu Gakko* 3:4 (1948): 42–45.

Ishihara, Tsuyoshi. "Sasaki Kuni to Metta Victoria Fuller Victor." *Eigo Seinen* 148:3 (2002): 198–99.

———. "20-seiki America Zasshi ni okeru Mark Twain-zo: Shoshiteki Kenkyu" *Doshisha American Studies* 39 (March 2003): 81–91.

Jingu, Teruo. "Sekai-teki Shiya no Naka deno Jido Bungaku." In *Nihon Jido Bungaku no Tokushoku,* ed. Teruo Jingu et al., 10–47. Tokyo: Meiji Shoin, 1974.

Jingu, Teruo, et al., eds. *Nihon Jido Bungaku no Tokushoku.* Tokyo: Meiji Shoin, 1974.

Kadono, Eiko. *Majo no Takkyubin.* Tokyo: Fukuinkan Shoten, 1985.

Kamei, Shunsuke. "Hikaku Bungaku: Nihon ni okeru Mark Twain." In *Koza Hikaku Bunka: Hikaku Bunka e no Tenbo,* ed. Shuntaro Ito, 173–201. Tokyo: Kenkyusha, 1977.

———. *Meriken kara Amerika e: Nichibei Bunka Koshoshi Oboegaki.* Tokyo: Tokyo Daigaku Shuppankai, 1979.

———. "Nihon no Kindai to Hon'yaku." In *Kindai Nihon no Hon'yaku Bunka,* ed. Shunsuke Kamei, 8–50. Tokyo: Chuokoronsha, 1994.

Kan, Tadamichi. *Nihon no Jido Bungaku.* Tokyo: Otsuki Shoten, 1966.

Kan, Takashi. Afterword to *Jido Bungaku to Shakai: Houkoku to Shinpojiumu,* ed. Teruo Jingu. Tokyo: Meiji Shoin, 1974.

Katsuura, Yoshio. *Hon'yaku no Konjaku: Mark Twain no Kotoba, Nihon-jin no Kotoba.* Hiroshima: Bunka Hyoron Shuppan, 1980.

———. *Nihon ni okeru Mark Twain: Gaisetsu to Bunken Mokuroku.* Tokyo: Kirihara Shoten, 1979.

———. "Nihon ni okeru Mark Twain." *Rissho Daigaku Kyoyobu Kiyo* 26 (1992): 47–65.

———. "Sasaki Kuni to Mark Twain no Sakuhin Hon'yaku." *Rissho Daigaku Kyoyobu Kiyo* 11 (1977): 53–62.

———. *Zoku Nihon ni okeru Mark Twain.* Tokyo: Kirihara Shoten, 1988.

Kawado, Michiaki, and Takanori Sakakibara, eds. *Mark Twain shu.* Vol. 20, *Meiji Hon'yaku Bungaku Zenshu Shimbun Zasshi hen.* Tokyo: Ozora sha, 1996.

Kawai, Saburo. "Nihon e no Hakushu." *Shonen Kurabu* 26:6 (1939): 106–23.

Kisaichi, Yasuhiko. "Nihon no Robinsonado: Shiken-yaku Jugo Shonen no Shuhen." In *Kindai Nihon no Hon'yaku Bunka,* ed. Shunsuke Kamei, 262–88. Tokyo: Chuokoronsha, 1994.

Kodansha. *Kodansha 70nen-shi, Sengo-hen.* Tokyo: Kodansha, 1985.

———. *Kodansha no 80 nen.* Tokyo: Kodansha, 1990.

Kokuritsu Kyouiku Kenkyujo Fuzoku Kyoiku Toshokan, ed. *Kokutei Kyokasho Naiyo Sakuin, Jinjo-ka Shushin Kokugo Shoka Hen: Kokutei Kyokasho Naiyo no Hensen.* Tokyo: Hiroike Gakuen Shuppanbu, 1966.

Kokuritsu Kyouiku Kenkyujo Fuzoku Kyouiku Toshokan and Kyokasho Kenkyu Center, ed. *Chugakko Kokugo Kyokasho Naiyo Sakuin, 1949–1986.* Tokyo: Tokyo Shoseki, 1986.

Kon, Madoko. "Amerika Kyouiku Shisetsudan no Okurimono." *Chuo Daigaku Bungakubu Kiyo, Shakaigakka* 6 (1996): 121–50.

Kosakai, Sumi. *Hyoden Sasaki Kuni: Humor Sakka no Ganso Koko ni Ari.* Tokyo: Themis, 2001.

Kunimatsu, Toshihide. "Motto Usuyogoreta Tom wo." *Nihon Jido Bungaku* 20:9 (July 1980): 44–47.

Kuwabara, Saburo. *Shonen Kurabu no Koro: Showa Zenki no Jido Bungaku.* Tokyo: Keio Tsushin, 1987.

Matsumoto, Masashi. *20-seiki Televi Tokuhon, Sekai Meisaku Gekijo Taizen.* Tokyo: Dobun Shoin, 1999.

Matsumoto, Takeshi. *Ryakudatsu Shita Bunka: Senso to Tosho.* Tokyo: Iwanami Shoten, 1993.

Miyazaki, Sanmai. "Oya no On." In *Shonen Bungaku,* vol. 10, ed. Sazanami Iwaya. Tokyo: Hakubunkan, 1892.

Muto, Teiichi. "Kotoshi wa Jugo Zentai no Senso da." *Shonen Kurabu* 26:1 (1939): 262–69.

———. "Tsuyoku Tadashiki Kuni ni Sakae Are." *Shonen Kurabu* 26:5 (1939): 310–11.

Nakagaki, Koutaro. "Abekobe no Sekai: Iwaya Sazanami hoka yaku *Shonen Shosetsu Kojiki Oji* to Nichibei Jido Bungaku no Dentou." *Horizon* 35 (2003): 65–79.

———. "Bungaku Kyouiku to Ideology: America Koten Jido Bungaku wo toushite saguru Nichibei Hikaku Bunka Kenkyu." *Waseda Review of Education* 18 (2004): 79–109.

———. "Kyoshitsu no naka no Huck Finn: Kyouiku Kyozai to shite no America Koten Bungaku wo Hikaku Bunka-teki ni Kousatsu suru." *Waseda Review of Education* 17 (2003): 55–68.

———. "*Tom Sawyer* no Humor wa Ikani Inyu saretaka: Sasaki Kuni ni yoru Mark Twain no Hon'yaku." *Horizon* 34 (2002): 28–43.

Nakamura, Mitsuo. "Senryoka no Bungaku." *Bungaku,* June 1952: 503–10.

———. "Warai no Soshitsu." In *Nakamura Mitsuo Zenshu,* 10:107–43. Tokyo: Chikuma Shobo, 1972.

Nakamura, Yuriko, and Taro Miura. "Senryoki ni okeru Kyouiku Shisetsudan karano 'Hon no Okurimono.'" *Toshokan Bunkashi Kenkyu* 18 (2001): 43–77.

Namekawa, Michio. *Nihon Jido Bungaku no Kiseki.* Tokyo: Rironsha, 1988.

Nasu, Yorimasa. "Nihon ni okeru Mark Twain." *Tabard* 11 (1996): 67–81.

Nihon Mark Twain Kyokai, ed., *Mark Twain: Kenkyu to Hihyo,* vol. 1. Tokyo: Nan'undo, 2002.

Nihon Shuppan Kyodo Kabushikigaisha, ed. *Nihon Shuppan Nenkan: Showa 19, 21-nen ban.* Tokyo: Nihon Shuppan Kyodo, 1947.

———. *Nihon Shuppan Nenkan: Showa 22, 23-nen ban.* Tokyo: Nihon Shuppan Kyodo, 1949.

———. *Shuppan Nenkan: Showa 17-nen ban.* Tokyo: Kyodo Shuppansha, 1942.

———. *Shuppan Nenkan: Showa 18-nen ban.* Tokyo: Kyodo Shuppansha, 1943.

Nishizaki, Yasuo. "Sasaki Kuni no Jido Bungaku: *Itazura Kozo Nikki* Kenkyu." *Kokusai Jido Bungakukan Kiyo* 13 (1998): 49–69.

Nissin Shokuhin Kabushikigaisha Shashi Hensanshitsu, ed. *Shokutarite Yo wa Tairaka.* Osaka: Nissin Shokuhin, 1992.

Nosaka, Akiyuki. "Hotaru no Haka." In *America Hijiki, Hotaru no Haka,* 57–86. Tokyo: Shinchosha, 1972.

Oe, Kenzaburo. "America Ryokosha no Yume: Jigoku ni Yuku Huckleberry Finn." *Sekai,* September 1966, 229–40.

———. "Huckleberry Finn to Hero no Mondai." In *Oe Kenzaburo Zen Sakuhinshu,* 2:351–66. Tokyo: Shinchosha, 1966.

———. "Shiiku." 1958. Reprint, in *Oe Kenzaburo Shosetsu,* 1:63–95. Tokyo: Shinchosha, 1996.

———. "Toni Morrison to Huckleberry Finn no Boken." *Asahi Shimbun,* March 11, 1997, Culture sec., evening ed.

Okawa, Etsuo, Kin'ya Katsuo, and Mikio Ando. "Zadankai: Hogen to Jido Bungaku." *Nihon Jido Bungaku* 26:3 (1980): 12–36.

Ono, Kosei. "Manga to Anime Nihon to Obei no Sogo Shinto: Ekkyou Suru Subculture." *Sekai* (May 1998): 258–63.

Osaragi, Jiro. *Bakumatsu Hishi: Kurama Tengu.* Tokyo: Hakubunkan, 1925.

———. *Dreyfus Jiken.* Tokyo: Tenjinsha, 1930.

———. *Kikyo.* Tokyo: Kurakusha, 1949.

———. *Muteki.* Tokyo: Shinchosha, 1934.

———. *Nadare.* Tokyo: Shinchosha, 1937.

———. *Pari Moyu.* Tokyo: Asahi Shimbunsha, 1964.

———. *Shijin.* Tokyo: Kurakusha, 1946.

———. *Shin Kurama Tengu: Jigoku Taiheiki.* Tokyo: Kofusha, 1966.

Oshikawa, Shunro. *Shin Nihon-jima.* Tokyo: Bunbudo, 1906.

Ota, Saburo. "Arishima Takeo 'Domomata no Shi.'" In *Kindai Sakka to Seiyo,* 66–91. Tokyo: Shimizu Kobundo, 1977.

———. "Mark Twain to Arishima Takeo: 'Domomata no Shi' wo meguru Mondai." In *Showa Women's College Eibei Bungaku Kiyo, Gakuen* 4 (1962): 22–36.

Russell, John G. *Nihonjin no Kokujin-kan.* Tokyo: Shinhyoron, 1991.

Sakanishi, Shiho. "Aisareru Shojo." In *Chugaku Shin Kokugo 1,* vol. 1, ed. Sanseido Henshujo, 96–107. Tokyo: Sanseido Shuppan, 1951.

Sasaki, Kuni. "Chintaro Nikki." 1920–1921. In *Sasaki Kuni Zenshu,* vol. 1, ed. Ozaki Hotsuki et al., 91–293. Tokyo: Kodansha, 1971.

———. *Good Boy Nikki.* Adapt. of *A Good Boy's Diary,* by Metta Victoria Fuller Victor. Tokyo: Naigai Shuppan Kyokai, 1910.

———. *Itazura Kozo Nikki.* Adapt. of *A Bad Boy's Diary,* by Metta Victoria Fuller Victor. Tokyo: Naigai Shuppan Kyokai, 1909.

———. "Kokusai Mark Twain Kyokai." In *Sasaki Kuni Zenshu,* vol. 10, ed. Ozaki Hotsuki et al., 346–48. Tokyo: Kodansha, 1975.

———. *Otenba Musume Nikki.* Adapt. of *A Naughty Girl's Diary,* by Metta Victoria Fuller Victor. Tokyo: Naigai Shuppan Kyokai, 1909.

———. *Tomu-kun Samu-kun.* 1933. In *Sasaki Kuni Zenshu,* vol. 9, ed. Ozaki Hotsuki et al., 447–529. Tokyo: Kodansha, 1975.

———. *Mura no Shonen-dan.* 1930–1932. In *Sasaki Kuni Zenshu,* vol. 9, ed. Ozaki Hotsuki et al., 277–443. Tokyo: Kodansha, 1975.

———, trans. *Mark Twain Meisaku Shu.* Tokyo: Kaizosha, 1929. Anthology of translations of Twain's works.

Sato, Tadao. "Shonen no Riso-shugi." 1959. In *Taishu Bunka no Genzo,* ed. Tadao Sato, 98–144. Tokyo: Iwanami Shoten, 1993.

Seki, Hideo. "Jido Bungaku sha wa Nani wo Nasubeki ka." *Nihon Jido Bungaku,* first issue (1946): 2–7.

———. "Minshushugi Jido Bungaku no 30-nen." In *Jido Bungaku no Sengoshi: Hyoron Nenpyo Nihon Jido Bungaku Somokuji,* ed. Hideo Seki et al., 10–47. Tokyo: Tokyo Shoseki, 1978.

Seki, Hideo, Mitsuo Ishikawa, and Tadamichi Kan. "Zadankai: Jido Bungaku wo Meguru Genron Yokuatsu no Rekishi." In *Nihon Jido Bungaku* 16:8 (1970): 68–88.

Sekiguchi, Yasuyoshi. "Nihon Jido Bungaku no Seiritsu: Shisoshi Shakaishi no Shiten kara." In *Jido Bungaku no Shisoshi Shakaishi,* ed. Nihon Jido Bungakkai, 11–43. Tokyo: Tokyo Shoseki, 1997.

Sekino, Yoshio, Yoshio Nakano, et al. "Hon'yaku Seishonen Tosho no Shomondai." *Seikatsu Gakko* 3:8 (1948): 2–14.

Shikata, Shin. "*Yadonashi Huck* no Nakamatachi no Koto." *Nihon Jido Bungaku,* May 1977: 70–71.

Shimada, Keizo. *Boken Dankichi Manga Zenshu.* Tokyo: Kodansha, 1967.

Shimazaki, Toson. *Hakai.* Tokyo: Uedaya, 1906.

Shinohara, Shigetoshi. *Shonen Shojo no tame no Minshu Tokuhon.* Tokyo: Kokumin Gakugeisha, 1947.

Sogo Josei-shi Kenkyukai, ed. *Nihon Josei no Rekishi, Shiso to Bunka: On'na to Otoko no Nozomashii Kankei wo Mezashite.* Tokyo: Kadokawa Shoten, 1993.

Sunada, Hiroshi. "'Eizo' ga Tsukuru 'Monogatari' to 'Kotoba' ga Tsukuru 'Monogatari.'" *Nihon Jido Bungaku* 41:2 (February 1995): 14–24.

Susukida, Kyukin. *Chabanashi.* Tokyo: Rakuyodo, 1916.

———. *Chabanashi Zenshu.* 2 vols. Osaka: Osaka Mainichi Shimbunsha, 1924.

———. *Nochi no Chabanashi.* Tokyo: Genbunsha, 1918.

———. *Shin Chabanashi.* Tokyo: Genbunsha, 1919.

Suzuki, Saeko. "Arishima Takeo 'Domomata no Shi' no Buntai to Kosei: Mark Twain tono Kankei ni tsuite." *Jissen Kokubungaku* 26 (1984): 55–65.

Takeda, Gyoten. "Nidai Chuko." In *Shonen Bungaku,* vol. 27, ed. Sazanami Iwaya. Tokyo: Hakubunkan, 1894.

Takeda, Toshio. "Furoji no Tanjo." *Jido* 2 (August 1947): 2–5.

Takita, Yoshiko. *American Life e no Manazashi: Shizen, Josei, Taishubunka.* Tokyo: Tokyo Daigaku Shuppankai, 2000.

Tanigawa, Takeshi. *Amerika Eiga to Senryo Seisaku.* Kyoto: Kyoto Daigaku Shuppan, 2002.

Tanji, Megumi. "Nihon ni okeru Mark Twain Kenkyu 'Mark Twain Studies in Japan.'" *Tokyo Daigaku Amerika Kenkyu Shiryo Center Nenpo* 15 (1993): 86–97.

Torigoe, Shin. "Boken Shosetsu no Miseijuku: Kaku Realism no Kanosei." In *Nihon Jido Bungaku no Tokushoku,* ed. Teruo Jingu et al., 221–51. Tokyo: Meiji Shoin, 1974.

———. *Nihon Jido Bungaku.* Tokyo: Kenpakusha, 1995.

———. "Sengo Jido Bungaku no 50-nen wo Gaikan Suru: Futatabi Meguttekita Kiki no Jidai no Naka de." In *Sengo Jido Bungaku no 50-nen,* ed. Shin Torigoe et al., 8–19. Tokyo: Bunkeido, 1996.

Torii, Fumiko. "Arishima Takeo 'Domomata no Shi' ni tsuite." *Jissen Bungaku* 10 (1960): 4–8.

Un'no, Jyuza. "Taiheiyo Raigeki Sentai." *Shonen Kurabu,* May 1933, 78–102.

Yamamoto, Taketoshi. *Senryoki Media Bunseki.* Tokyo: Hosei Daigaku Shuppankyoku, 1996.

Yanagita, Kunio. "Warai no Bungaku no Kigen." In *Teihon Yanagita Kunio Shu,* 7:153–73. Tokyo: Chikuma Shobo, 1962.

———, ed. *Atarashii Kokugo Chugaku 3-nen,* vol. 1. Tokyo: Tokyo Shoseki, 1954.

Yano, Tetsu. *Kamui no Ken.* Tokyo: Kadokawa Shoten, 1975.

Yoshikawa, Eiji. "*Miyamoto Musashi.*" *Asahi Shimbun,* August 23, 1930–May 20, 1932, January 1, 1933–July 11, 1934, evening ed.

Yoshitake, Yoshitaka. "Arishima Takeo no Hon'an-geki 'Domomata no Shi.'" In *Kindai Bungaku no Naka no Seiō,* 245–52. Tokyo: Kyoiku Shuppan Center, 1974.

Films

For Japanese film adaptations of Twain and U.S. films distributed in Japan, see appendix.

U.S. Film Adaptations of Twain's Works

The Adventures of Huck Finn. Dir. Stephen Sommers, Walt Disney Pictures, 1993.

The Adventures of Huckleberry Finn. Dir. Richard Thorpe, MGM, 1939.

The Adventures of Huckleberry Finn. Dir. Michael Curtiz, MGM, 1960.

The Adventures of Huckleberry Finn. Dir. Lee Thompson, United Artists–Reader's Digest, 1975.

Adventures of Huckleberry Finn. Dir. Peter H. Hunt, Great Amwell Company/PBS, 1985.

The Adventures of Tom Sawyer. Dir. Norman Taurog, United Artists, 1938.

Huckleberry Finn. Dir. Robert Totten, Pictures International, ABC, 1975.

Mark Twain's Tom Sawyer. Dir. Don Taylor, United Artists–Reader's Digest, 1973.

Tom and Huck. Dir. Peter Hewitt, Walt Disney Pictures, 1995.

English Versions of Japanese Animes

The Adventures of Tom and Huck. 105 min., Woodland Hills, CA: Celebrity Home Entertainment, 1995.

The All New Adventures of Tom Sawyer: "Full Speed Ahead." 60 min., Woodland Hills, CA: Celebrity Home Entertainment, 1991.

The All New Adventures of Tom Sawyer: Mischief on the Mississippi. 95 min., Woodland Hills, CA: Celebrity Home Entertainment, 1991.

The All New Adventures of Tom Sawyer: Pain the Day Away. 95 min., Woodland Hills, CA: Celebrity Home Entertainment, 1991.

The All New Adventures of Tom Sawyer: "Pirates and Caves and Ghosts—Oh, My!" 60 min., Woodland Hills, CA: Celebrity Home Entertainment, 1991.

The All New Adventures of Tom Sawyer: No School for Pirates. 30 min., Woodland Hills, CA: Celebrity Home Entertainment, 1992.

The Raft Adventures of Huck & Jim. 72 min., Three B Productions, 1984.

Non-Twain Japanese Animes

Ace wo Nerae! Scen. Remika Yamamoto, TBS, Tokyo Movie, October 5, 1973–March 29, 1974.

Attack No. 1. Dir. Fumio Kurokawa and Eiji Okabe, scen. Chikako Urano, Fuji Television Network, Tokyo Movie, December 7, 1969–November 28, 1971.

Candy Candy, scen. Yumiko Igarashi, TV Asahi, Toei Doga, October 1, 1976–February 2, 1979.

Hotaru no Haka. Dir. Isao Takahata, Studio Ghibli, Toho, 1988.

Mahotsukai Sally. Scen. Mitsuteru Yokoyama, Asahi Hoso, Toei Doga, December 5, 1966–December 30, 1968.

Majo no Takkyubin. Dir. Hayao Miyazaki, Studio Ghibli, Toei, 1989.

Mononoke Hime. Dir. Hayao Miyazaki, Studio Ghibli, 1997.

Sailor Moon. Scen. Naoko Takeuchi, TV Asahi, Toei Agency, March 7, 1992–February 27, 1993.

Sen to Chihiro no Kamikakushi. Dir. Hayao Miyazaki, Studio Ghibli, 2001.

Index

Page numbers in italics refer to illustrations.

About the Author

Tsuyoshi Ishihara is teaching American Literature and Culture at Waseda University in Tokyo, Japan.